ON THE CUSP

The Women of Penn '64

**STORIES OF 19
UNIVERSITY OF
PENNSYLVANIA WOMEN
IN THE VANGUARD
OF CHANGING
WOMEN'S ROLES
IN BUSINESS,
THE PROFESSIONS,
ACADEMIA, AND
SOCIETY AT LARGE**

by Anne Sceia Klein
Wharton '64 & Annenberg '65

and Vilma Barr

D1365306

First Edition, 2018

ISBN-13: 978-0692082317 (standard paperback – photos in black & white)
ISBN-13: 978-1732101302 (deluxe paperback – most photos in color)
ISBN-13: 978-1732101319 (ebook - mobi version)
ISBN-13: 978-1732101326 (ebook – epub version)

Library of Congress Control Number: 2018936362

Pine Road Press
Medford, NJ 08055

What readers are saying about *ON THE CUSP*

The women's voices in this excellent and engaging volume provide not only a captivating window into their experiences as Penn students "on the cusp" of second-wave feminism (late '60s-early '70s), but also valuable insights that resonate in today's era of the "#Me Too" and "#Times Up" movements.

> *Michael X. Delli Carpini*
> *Dean, Annenberg School for Communication*
> *University of Pennsylvania*

A very timely and insightful read into the lives of extraordinary women enrolled at Penn in the 1960s. Each story shows true grit, determination and a drive to succeed in a male-dominated society, shedding light on a valuable but underappreciated part of Penn's history and culture. I found the stories inspirational. The sacrifices and the perseverance of these women would make them wonderful role models for many generations to come.

> *Rahul Kapoor*
> *Associate Professor of Management*
> *The Wharton School, University of Pennsylvania*

As a "double Penn" (College for Women '69 and Law School '76), I was fascinated to read *On the Cusp*. Those of us in college in the late sixties experienced the change from coffee dates to sit-ins and from Pappagallo flats to hiking boots, but I don't think we had enough knowledge of and appreciation for the women who came immediately before us. The stories of the Women of Penn '64 provide a first-hand narrative of the lives and careers of these women. I am in awe of their dreams and their achievements, and I am eternally grateful. The book paints a vivid portrait of society at that moment in time and of the individual lives of each of the women profiled. I couldn't put the book down. I wanted to know as much as possible about each of these pioneers. They make me proud to be one of the women of Penn.

> *Kathleen O'Brien, Esq.*
> *Partner, Montgomery McCracken Walker & Rhoads LLP*
> *Philadelphia*

The book recounts a cohort of women from the Penn Class of 1964 who pushed through the "way things were" to the next level of change and transition in society. The women's stories are interesting and engaging.

> *Gregory E. Johnson, CFP®*
> *Director of Gift Planning*
> *University of Pennsylvania*

Anne Klein has written a truly inspirational book, honestly relating how 19 "can do" women, encouraged by strong, supportive parents, often first-generation immigrants or GI Bill veterans, and a first-class education at Penn, brought about social and economic change in the USA. It is one of the best mentoring-by-example books that I have read. The message of Anne's book is that Penn gives its students two things: knowledge and confidence to think the unthinkable. How true.

Lady Anne Foff Judge (Wharton Graduate School '75)
Co-founder, The Judge Business School, University of Cambridge
London, England

So many of the personal stories were really touching, even for me as a millennial male. I'd really like to show the completed work to my mother and aunts since they have always been very education-focused women. My mother has her own stories about being an African-American woman trying to break into the journalism field in the early 1970s and my paternal great-grandfather insisted that his daughter, my grandmother, go to college (in the 1940s) so that she "would never have to depend on a man to take care of her."

Timothy H. Horning
Public Services Archivist
University of Pennsylvania

I found the book incredibly insightful. As a millennial, I had no idea of the challenges that were present for women during the '60s and '70s. I can't thank you and your classmates enough, and all the women who fought and paved the way, so that my generation could take advantage of the opportunities that have been given to us. I will see you and your classmates as my role models.

Bettina Hauser
ALDI Store Operations Area Manager
Dublin, Ireland

The extraordinary women profiled here were in the forefront of changes in the status of women that have taken place over the past 50-plus years. Through their personal proactive determination, they became role models for their daughters and others to emulate.

Stanley W. Silverman
Founder & CEO, Silverman Leadership
Columnist, American Business Journals
Former President & CEO, PQ Corp.

The Women of Penn '64 is a collection of personal narratives by University of Pennsylvania women who received their degrees and entered the workforce as they faced challenges in career paths that prioritized the male. These are feisty women who recount personal stories from childhood to retirement and who demonstrate determination to succeed — and achieve enormous success — in the corporate and non-profit sectors, law, medicine, scientific research and academia.

Dr. Susan K. Leshnoff (College for Women '67)
Distinguished Professor Emerita
College of Communication and the Arts
Seton Hall University

What a remarkable account of the lives and careers of these women from the University of Pennsylvania 1964. These stories are both moving and inspiring. In a world where far more opportunities were available to men than ever were to women, these stories are a tangible demonstration of the courage and desire women had at that time to follow their dreams and succeed in their chosen careers. Anne and Vilma have captured the very essence of the true courage women showed in the '60s, reaching the top of their chosen professions under great hardship. Well done. It's a must read for all young women…and men too, for that matter.

John Wells
Chairman, Wells Haslem Mayhew Strategic Public Affairs
Sydney, Australia

As society strides towards greater equality of opportunity, career women must continue to demonstrate that they are equal to the task of matching their male counterparts in all aspects of work, management and leadership. In *On the Cusp*, they can draw inspiration from the experiences of the Women of Penn '64, and go forth boldly to make a difference.

Yap Boh Tiong
Chairman, The Mileage Communications Group
Headquarters: Singapore

We have told our five grown daughters (all educated and employed) about the book and they can't wait to read it. Every parent with a daughter should get a copy of this book, then read it and discuss it together.

Bob and Barbara Barrall
Medford, NJ

Dedications

To my husband, Gerhart L. (Jerry) Klein, Esq., for his love and indulgence as I worked on this book for more than a year. Sincere gratitude to him for his editing and layout skills, as he spent countless hours helping Vilma and me prepare the manuscript with innumerable drafts and photographs from classmates. — *Anne Sceia Klein*

To my brother, Stephen D. Leshnoff, School of Engineering '66, and my sister-in-law, Dr. Susan Leshnoff, College for Women '67. Their individual careers represent exceptional achievements in their chosen fields of science and engineering, and art and art education, respectively. — *Vilma Barr*

Acknowledgements

Our sincerest thanks to the Penn Alumni Relations Staff for all their assistance and encouragement as we wrote this book. Our special thanks to

• Hoopes F. Wampler, Associate Vice President

• Lisbeth Willis, Director, Classes & Reunions

• Greg Johnson, Director of Gift Planning

• Kathleen Margay, Development & Alumni Relations, Penn Medicine

Thanks also to: Mark Frazier Lloyd and Tim Horning, Penn archivists; Penn Professor emeritus Klaus Krippendorf; Rowan University professor Paul Eisenberg; The College of New Jersey Professor Larry Litwin; Donna Greenberg; and thanks to all the other friends who provided commentaries.

Most of all, thanks to The Women of Penn '64 for their willingness to be interviewed and their cooperation in editing their texts and providing their photos. Without them, this book would not exist. Any errors in recounting their stories is wholly our fault, not theirs.

Photos of the subjects were provided by them.

Portrait of Judith Ross Berkowitz courtesy of Capehart Photography.

University of Pennsylvania photos used with permission.

I fought the battles of the sixties
Which you recall were rather draining
When men were thick I hit the fray
Became a prick, Got equal pay
I faced down chauvinistic slobs
I won the fights, improved the jobs
And, oh, I'm not complaining
                    …
I find that getting work is harder
Each job I want takes more campaigning
And those sweet young things who hire me now
Those MBAs making fifty thou
Who smile and ask what I have done
When they got their jobs from the fights I won…
But I'm not complaining

Table of Contents

Foreword by Dr. Amy Gutmann
President, University of Pennsylvania

Dr. Amy Gutmann is the eighth President of the University of Pennsylvania, serving since 2004. She is an internationally renowned leader in higher education and a prominent advocate for increased access to higher education, for innovation based on interdisciplinary collaboration, and for the transformative impact of universities, locally, nationally and globally. In November 2016, Penn announced President Gutmann's contract had been extended to 2022, making her the longest-serving president in Penn's history. In her 2004 inaugural address, President Gutmann outlined a bold and ambitious vision for the University: the Penn Compact. Penn's commitment to the three core values of the Penn Compact – Inclusion, Innovation and Impact – has propelled the University forward during an era of dramatic change.

On the Cusp: The Women of Penn '64 chronicles the journeys of 19 remarkable women. And, as with all good books, it leaves a lasting impression. You will empathize with their struggles, laugh with their discoveries, applaud their courage, and reflect on how much we take for granted today. These women dared to be different, not because they set out to be pioneers, but because they asked questions that societal and cultural norms dictated they should not. They gave themselves the freedom to find answers by pursuing personal and professional goals and became trendsetters for those following in their footsteps on Penn's campus and beyond.

Each of *The Women of Penn '64* embraced challenges and effectively navigated transitions on their road to success. The only woman in a classroom full of men or entering a male-dominated field. The science major who became an entrepreneur. The English literature enthusiast who would garner executive appointments from two U.S. presidents. *The Women of Penn '64* are engineers, educators, physicians, community activists, designers, and much more. They forged paths when there were no maps. And today, each woman stands as a testament of fortitude, character, and wisdom.

While there is a recurring theme that the University of Pennsylvania gave something to each of these women, one can easily flip that coin to see what these women continually give back to Penn. *On the Cusp: The Women of Penn '64* encourages you to dive into the unknown with a fearless tenacity and inspires you to dream again.

Preface

It all began when the University of Pennsylvania undergraduate Class of 1964 came together for its 50th anniversary reunion. Many of the female classmates told incredible stories about the obstacles they faced during their journeys into the worlds of business, law, medicine, science, government and public service. Each woman thought her story was unique to her. As the story-telling progressed, everyone realized they were not alone in their experiences. No one had ever shared their stories. We realized it was time to document them.

In *On the Cusp*, Anne Sceia Klein and Vilma Barr tell the stories of 19 women of the Penn Class of 1964 who had few, if any, female role models to follow. They achieved success on their own, with no career path and little guidance to help develop their talents. Feminism, the glass ceiling, networking and female entrepreneurship were unknown concepts in the 1960s. Yet these women broke molds and blazed trails.

The women interviewed for this book were children of the "Silent Generation." They came from Pennsylvania, New York, New Jersey and Delaware. With careers and marriages, these same women found their way to California, Texas, New Mexico, Colorado, Georgia, Florida, Massachusetts, Connecticut and Washington, D.C.

Their experiences, seen together here, are the previously undocumented — and unrecognized — achievements that signaled the start of profound changes in American society.

Anne Sceia Klein
(Wharton 1964, Annenberg School for Communication 1965)

Vilma Barr

Introduction

The Rise of Women's Leadership and the Role of the University of Pennsylvania

The University of Pennsylvania attracts students from all over the world and from all different backgrounds. While the women enrolled at Penn in the early 1960s didn't recognize it at the time, they were gaining real-life experience in seeing and working with students who were unlike themselves.

Most of these women were not exposed to other successful career women in their classes; yet, they cited the opportunities Penn offered outside of the classroom as invaluable — organizational events, sports, staff positions on the *Daily Pennsylvanian* and other publications, and student government.

The women were unanimous in their praise that Penn provided an excellent education, bolstering confidence among the women as they set forth into the world. Professors were named as inspirational, and many contributed greatly to a "well-rounded" education in history, music, art and religious thought, among others. Nearly all the women remembered being told they were the "best and the brightest," though no one could remember exactly where she heard the comment.

No one worried much about "dressing for success," since Penn women in the 1960s could not wear pants outside of their dormitories — they had to be "dressed" for class and in the dining room as well. Many remembered the pleated

Typical women's dress in the mid-sixties.
(Penn Archives photo)

skirts, knee socks, Bass Weejun loafers, and crew neck sweaters. Dressing for sorority meetings (and even movie dates) was expected to involve high heels and nylon stockings.

The women remember a few incidents of what today is known as harassment, but they tactfully shut down the off-color conversations and the inappropriate behaviors as soon as they began. There also were instances of discrimination, such as not being allowed to take a statistics class, and not being able to get a B. S. degree in chemistry without taking several semesters of additional courses beyond the normal graduation requirements for the College for Women. The physicians noted women composed only 10 percent of their class. There were no women cheerleaders nor women in the marching band. But Penn was way ahead of other Ivy League Schools with men and women in classes.

The new dormitory — at the time called the New Residence Hall (opened in January 1961) — offered additional experiences for the women, as nearly every woman who lived on the campus recalled her first semester of dorm living, being scattered at various women's dormitories around the campus.

The first Dean of Women of the College for Women was appointed in 1960. She is generally remembered as suggesting teaching careers to many of our interviewees. But the 1960s marked the beginning of women majoring in fields other than teaching and nursing. The women of the Class of 1964 were exceptional — smart, curious and motivated. They took classes in fields not traditionally pursued by women, even though their mothers had encouraged them to obtain a "teaching certificate, just in case...."

The women entering the workplace in 1964 were not welcomed by most of the men in their fields. They faced tremendous odds against success, yet they were determined to succeed. Although the times were very different in the 1960s, the University of Pennsylvania recognized that society and education were changing, and provided the foundation for women to excel in roles that led to the "Rise in Women's Leadership."

On the Cusp of Change: The Women of Penn '64

The women graduates of the University of Pennsylvania's class of 1964 came to its West Philadelphia campus at the beginning of a decade marked by extreme change and great drama in American history. Their daily lives would be affected by the overlapping swirl of shifting patterns — from social to scientific — that became evident in the late postwar 1950s.

These were smart and talented women from the tops of their high school classes. Many received University scholarships, Mayoral and Senatorial Scholarships, and scholarships from outside organizations. Penn's administrators told them during their orientation they were among the "the best and the brightest." What they were not advised was that once they got their degrees, they would be entering into a society not yet fully committed to accept them as equals in business, the professions, in medicine or science. (No criticism of Penn intended; it's difficult to analyze history when it is being made.)

The 19 women profiled here had no precedent of role models on which to base their future careers. Women in high places were few and far between when the Women of Penn '64 matriculated. Other than Margaret Chase Smith of Maine, who served as a U.S. Representative (1940–49) and a U.S. Senator (1949–73); Dorothy Chandler, Los Angeles cultural leader; and Katharine Graham, who headed *The Washington Post*, other examples are hard to find. Yet, the experiences of the women documented in this book are histories of determination and intelligence which, when combined with their Penn education, created personal success stories. The women represent an exponential growth into the present when women now are running some of the largest multi-billion-dollar companies in the world.

- The Baby Boomers, male and female, came of age in the 1960s and ballooned college attendance. A new system of mass higher education stemmed from the GI Bill's education entitlements and public funding of research. The number of women attending and graduating from college kept growing through the 1950s, prompting educators to predict an "impending tidal wave of students" would hit campuses around 1960.

- Spurred by the fears of falling behind in technology — given Russia's success with Sputnik — the U.S. government increased its funding directed to the University of Pennsylvania and other institutions of higher education. To take advantage of these grants, colleges and universities geared up to handle a major jump in applications. In the years between 1960 and 1970, enrollments more than doubled. A third of high school graduates went on to college, as male and female graduates from more middle-class and working-class families became part of student bodies around the country.

The trend was notable at the University of Pennsylvania. In 1964, the number of women who graduated from the College for Women and the Wharton School numbered 385. Of the 19 women profiled in this book, six went on directly to graduate schools and professional training. Thirteen accepted positions in business and industry, but six of those did seek graduate degrees later on.

Most of the contributors to this book reported their awareness of a higher pay scale for men performing the same job as they held. For the most part, fear of reprisal kept them from taking action to report the discrepancy. Maternity leave did not exist.

- **More than half of the U.S. 1960 population of 181 million were women. Betty Friedan's *The Feminine Mystique* sold three million copies in the three years following its publication in 1963.**

- Friedan argued that regardless of talent and education, women were largely treated as second-class citizens. They were expected to make coffee and take minutes of meetings, no matter how much experience they had serving in leadership roles in volunteer organizations or the high quality of college education they received. Friedan urged women to see themselves differently as strong and independent, acquiring the power and freedom to determine their own lives.

Trends toward the emancipation of women after the mid-1950s were marked by the rising proportions of women in salaried work, increased college attendance, emphasis on women's self-fulfillment in careers and more egalitarian ideas of marriage. By the early 1960s, published works by eminent sociologists called attention to the status of women and the promise of gender equality. Among other topics, they examined the slow progress of changing roles in family decision-making, where male dominance was seen as still in place.

- **Federal funding of university research doubled in the last half of the 1950.**

- By the time the Women of Penn '64 finished their studies, research money was reaching a six-fold growth rate. Examples of emerging applied technology were evident when Digital Equipment Corporation in 1963 introduced the first minicomputer. In 1965, Erna Schneider Hoover of Bell Laboratories developed and patented the first computer software to switch telephone calls, forming the basis for the country's electronic switching system.

• On July 2, just a few weeks after the class of 1964 graduated, President Lyndon Johnson signed the Civil Rights Acts of 1964 and established the Equal Employment Opportunity Commission (EEOC).

• The Civil Rights Act and the EEOC formalized in law the recognition of equal rights and initiatives for women and for minorities. It was the start of an era when change in accepting women as equals in the workplace would be very slowly encouraged and even more slowly accepted. Even as this book is being written (2017), many women still believe there is a difference in how men and women are treated in the workplace; they believe women are not seen as serious contenders.

• **Beginnings of counterculture were evident, starting on the West Coast.**

• The mid to late Sixties saw the rise of the civil rights movement, the anti-Vietnam War movement, the women's movement, the environmental movement and the gay rights movement. Supporters of these movements questioned traditional practices about how people were treated. Why did black and white children attend separate schools, and why were women prevented from holding certain jobs? This questioning inspired people to begin organizing movements to fight for equal rights for all people. But these movements did not really fully emerge until after the Penn women of the class of 1964 had graduated.

• Students in Penn's dorms and lounges watched as television news reported the tense Bay of Pigs crisis as it unfolded in April of 1961 and the Cuban Missile crisis in October, 1962.

• Rachel Carson's *Silent Spring,* published in 1962, laid the foundation for the Save the Environment movement. John Glenn orbited the earth in the same year.

• John F. Kennedy was assassinated on November 22, 1963. President Lyndon Johnson, on May 22,1964, announced his Great Society agenda, dealing with poverty, urban blight, and education.

• Protests against the Vietnam War were staged on college campuses and organized in populated urban areas, but not until *after* the 1964 graduation.

The Women of Penn '64 linked their own energy levels to the forces driving the modernization of social behavior, re-evaluation of gender roles, and the grasp of the process of striving for and assuming decision-making power. They were there at the beginning. They did not hook on to a widespread women's movement, as that phenomenon had not yet occurred.

Rather, an inner drive instilled by being part of "the best and the brightest" propelled them. They came from different places. From the University of Pennsylvania, the women took away their own interpretation of personal achievement, for the common good, for their immediate friends and family, and for themselves.

References:

The Changing Face of American Society: 1945-2000, Christopher Collier and James Lincoln Collier,. Benchmark Books, 2002

A Cultural History of the United States: The 1960s, Gini Holland, Lucent Books Inc. 1999

Age of Contradiction: American Thought and Culture in the 1960s, Howard Brick, Twayne Publishers, 1998

Overcoming the Challenges

By Anne Sceia Klein W64 ASC65

For the women who graduated in the Class of 1964, challenge is a fascinating theme. Few of us were encouraged to pursue a career. There was a lot of social pressure to find a spouse before graduation.

Gender wasn't a topic even discussed because nobody was aware of or even acknowledged gender differences at the time. Women still had "their place." Our class began breaking some long-standing molds of the place of women in the economy and began moving ahead. Our education was so good, and we were incredibly confident we could do anything, even though most of us didn't yet know where we were going to land once we graduated.

We had so many obstacles to overcome, primarily the traditional male dominance in our chosen career fields. For us, it was "the way it was." We rarely recognized that when we hit a wall, it was there because of our gender.

There was no noticeable change in the work environment for women with education and ability to get ahead in management until women started to push down the walls and the barriers to advancement. The early feminists created awareness. They were savvy and smart, but the business world had not changed enough to accept them.

We needed to learn how to "play the game" in business. We realized we were smart and could do the work, but we also had to "look" the part—do everything to gain stature and be accepted. We learned "boardroom" behavior; no one ever taught us, and men took advantage of our lack of knowledge.

The intervening years—a little more than a half-century—have witnessed a near-miracle in the status of women in leadership roles, with some women now directing multi-billion dollar multi-national corporations.

None of us women in the Penn class of '64 made it to the CEO level in a major corporation. The environment for that progress to happen hadn't been formed. Yet, many of us whose careers have led us to reach out and influence the lives of others feel the same sense of achievement. We became CEOs of our own companies. Our scale might have been smaller, but the quality of purpose and its realization can be appreciated and admired in the lives of the women we have documented here.

Like the pioneers, we cut the roads so other women could follow.

Changing Times

In the late 1960s and early 1970s, when women started to be hired in professional roles, rather than only staff support positions, particular issues arose.

Dating a Colleague in the Workplace

Men and women employed together were not allowed to date each other, even though both might have been working 60 to 80 hours a week. Sneaking around did not contribute to building a stable relationship. After a while, these decisions were reversed, but if a couple was "seriously dating," they had to tell a partner in the professional firm to avoid sexual harassment charges.

Married Coworkers

How should a man and a woman who were married be treated in the workplace? The decision in many business and professional firms was that only one of the married couple could be hired. So the couple had to choose which one would join or stay at the firm because the other one could not.

Business Travel

There was quite a protest against women being allowed to travel with married men. Married women wanted to travel with their husbands to keep them from "straying." Wives did their best to keep working women from getting ahead. Slowly, business women won the right to travel since travel was a typical business requirement for many business women. They were very smart in how they related to the businessmen they traveled with, and life went on.

What Women Could Not Do 50 Years Ago

Sarah Friedman, writing in the summer of 2017, noted there were several things women could not do 50 years ago, among them:

- Serve on a jury
- Get a credit card in her own name
- Run the Boston Marathon
- Keep her job if she became pregnant
- Attend a military academy or fight in combat
- Take legally mandated maternity leave
- For the complete list, see https://www.bustle.com/p/13-simple-things-women-couldnt-do-50-years-ago-in-the-us-66601

All-Male Clubs

In the mid-1960s, most major American cities had private clubs that were open only to male membership. It was a tradition harking back to the men's clubs of 18th century London. In some instances, women could enter the clubs, but only when accompanied by a member. When they could enter, women often were not allowed to use the main entrance, but could enter only through a separate door at the side or rear, or through the ground floor or basement.

The tide gradually began to change as more and more women entered the business world. It became impossible to ignore the fact that these clubs were places where businessmen discussed business. Excluding women from those conversations denied them opportunities for success and advancement; the "old boys' network" deprived women of access to the inner circles of power where decisions were made.

The change began with the Ivy League university alumni clubs. The Princeton Club admitted women in 1963, the Yale Club in 1969, and the Harvard Club in 1973. Gradually, as anti-discrimination sentiment and laws grew, private clubs across major cities including New York, Philadelphia, Baltimore, Detroit, Chicago and Los Angeles were forced to change their policies. Then a series of Supreme Court rulings in the 1980s narrowed the definition of "private clubs." Prohibitions against discrimination on the basis of sex, race or religion began to be applied more broadly. Clubs affected included university clubs, service clubs (e.g. Jaycees, Rotary, Lions and Kiwanis) and Union League clubs, among others.

In 1986, most clubs acted to admit women just ahead of the legislation which would have forced their membership policies to change. Many club presidents acknowledged the decision to admit women also reflected the fact that many members and their companies slowly had stopped paying dues. As more women and minorities were accepted, the clubs' financial situation began to turn around.

Thanks to Ilene Leff, Penn Class of 1964, for her assistance with this section of the book.

The Women of Penn '64

The chapters that follow are based on in-person or telephone interviews with each of the women.

Judith Roth Berkowitz

Rev. Dr. Betty Martin-Blount

Camille Quarrier Bradford, Esq.

Rona Solomon Cohen

Sandra Lotz Fisher

Leslie Mesnick Gallery-Dilworth

Claire Israel Gordon

Eda L. Hochgelerent, M.D.

Susan Miller Hoffman

Constance McNeely Horner

Marion Sokal Hubing, Esq.

Neen (Esther) Schwartz Hunt

Anne Sceia Klein

Ilene Leff

Faye C. Natanblut Laing, M.D.

Ruth Wolff Fields Messersmith

Patricia McLaughlin Nicosin

Andrea Pilch

Barbara Schepps Wong, M.D.

JUDITH BERKOWITZ

ENTREPRENEUR AND
FORMER PENN TRUSTEE

Women in our class were given an opportunity they never had before. Penn was our ticket to the world. And we took advantage of it. We were smart. We knew we had an opportunity, and we took it. We were an amazing group of women.

We didn't know what we were in for when we went into the workplace. I don't think any of us realized it, but we found there were people who didn't want us to be there. We actually had no previously recognized place. So, we made a place and just plowed ahead. Making our own way was quite difficult, but we did it.

Judith Roth Berkowitz

My Early Years

I grew up in Far Rockaway, in Queens, N.Y. Far Rockaway High School was like many schools at the time; it had multiple tracks based on scholastic ability. I was in the advanced track with 30 other students. Many of our teachers were veterans returning from World War II who had gone to college on the G.I. Bill, and they were very good instructors. Our advanced group of talented scholars was aware that we were given special treatment. We were prepared to go on to a good college.

 Sadly, my mother had to leave school after graduating from high school. It was the Depression, and she had to go to work. Later, she suffered a tragic setback when my father unexpectedly died of a heart attack at age 45, leaving her a widow with three children: I was seven, with a ten-year-old brother and 18-month-old sister. Still, she was determined her children would get a higher education. We studied hard and received good grades in high school, but we knew if we were going to college, we needed to get scholarships. My brother Paul went to Harvard and then to Harvard Law. My sister went to Boston University. I received a scholarship from the Green Bus Lines and Penn. I don't think I had any other plans besides getting an education. I didn't know exactly what I planned to be, so I didn't have an overwhelming drive to do something specific. My mother wanted me to be a teacher. Back in the 1960s, women became teachers or nurses, but I didn't want to do either.

My mother was one of those people who really believed if you took what you were given and worked as hard as you could, you could make things happen, and she was a perfect example. After my father's death, she had to find a way to make a living to keep her family together; she opened a women's clothing store in the basement of our house. She looked in the phonebook, found the nice streets in Far Rockaway, and she would send out postcards inviting the women to visit her in our basement. I saw how you can do something if you set your mind to it. I did clothing alterations as I got older. I can still sew a perfect hem! One of the great lessons in life is when you work hard for something, you can get there. In my mother's case, her goal was raising a family, keeping us together and making sure we all got an education. She succeeded.

When my brother got a scholarship to Harvard and went away, my mother's relatives tolerated this extravagance. When I did the same thing, they were miserable because they said, "Why would you put that money into a girl's education?" My mother said, "Because she deserves it." My mother never had those opportunities, and she wanted me to have them. She was convinced if I got them, things would work out, and she was right.

Let me tell you a little more about my background.

Choosing a Major
When I entered Penn in 1960, you could take as many courses as you wanted. I kept dropping and adding classes. The University offered some resistance, but finally gave up and let me take the classes. Everything was possible at Penn. It still is. You just have to look harder and work harder for what you want now, because everything is done school-by-school.

As a scholarship student determined to learn as much as I could, I took six or seven courses a semester. It was a tremendous opportunity for me. At one point, when I told my advisor I want to go into science, he tried to talk me out of it, telling me my math skills were not strong enough. Nevertheless, I took biology. In those days, biology was the one class used to flunk out the students who wanted to go to medical school but weren't going to make it. It was a very, very hard course. You actually couldn't pass it unless you had taken chemistry and physics, but I had been in the accelerated classes at Far Rockaway where we took four years of science. I did well, B+. To this day I remember that killer class and seeing students crying all around me when they received failing grades.

I continued to take science and took the first course in genetics offered at Penn; it was on the discovery of DNA. The women in our class who went on to be physicians or major in chemistry found that Penn wasn't quite as helpful as it could've been, but those were the times. There was still a lot of hesitancy to recognize women and let them get to where they wanted to be...where they are today.

Financing My Education

When my brother drove me to school, he showed me how to open a bank account. I'll never forget the bank officer asked if we had the $100 minimum needed to open an account, so I whispered to my brother, "What do we have?" He said to me, "We have only $10." We told the bank officer, "We only have $10. If you don't open the account, we'll go to another bank." The bank opened the account!

When tuition doubled the following year, luckily Penn increased my support. I also worked jobs for my room and board, including gigs in the admissions office, as a legal secretary and in a very short-lived stint waiting tables—I lasted only one shift!

At Penn, money was never the judge of success. When I got to Penn, no one knew me. No one knew if I was a scholarship student or not. No one asked; no one cared. The people I became friendly with didn't know I was a scholarship recipient and vice versa. As I got older, I found out I was one of the few scholarship students. To me, it was an eye-opening experience that nobody cared. You just made your friends based on whom you liked and thought was a terrific person, and you took the courses you wanted to take. Nobody got special attention for being wealthier than somebody else or for having a scholarship. These were great lessons.

My background gave me a tremendous opportunity because I understood what hardship was; many of the other students at Penn had no idea. It gave me tremendous confidence when the Dean of Women also understood that. She said to me, "You can come to me with any of your problems, and we'll talk about it." I never went back to see her, because she already had given me the best advice in our first meeting. "You just take your background, and you make it work for you in whatever way you can." That insight helped me to appreciate all the teachers and the many interested people who helped me along the way.

Thank you, Penn

While there were ups and downs during my college years, Penn prepared me for every opportunity that came my way. One of the reasons I stayed so active at Penn is I always felt Penn gave me the grounding, the background and the ability to do everything I subsequently was able to do.

I vividly remember one of the "downs." The first day of class, I went to my statistics class and arrived a little late because the class was all the way across campus. When I walked into the room, the professor stopped class, looked at me and said, "What are you looking for?" "Statistics," was my response. He said, "This is statistics." "So I just take a seat, correct?" He said, "I think you're in the wrong place." I looked around the classroom and saw no other girls in the class; I left. This experience was not an encouraging beginning.

The response in my Symphony class was quite different. When I realized I was the only one in the class who had never taken music lessons or been to a symphony, I panicked and approached my instructor. He told me not to worry, he would help me...and he did.

I received a phenomenal education at Penn. In all my future endeavors, my Penn education gave me the chance to take advantage of the opportunities that came my way. Coming from my background, exposure at Penn was everything — seeing how people had opportunities and how they could take advantage of them.

Penn gave me confidence. It helped me understand that I could do all the things I wanted to do; I've never doubted my education was a good one. Although I received a Bachelor of Science degree in Education, I never taught but used my education background to become involved in a New York City education non-profit which I helped found and still chair.

I met my husband, Howard, Wharton '62, at Penn. He was from Indiana and also believed his Penn education helped him to achieve professional success. We both stayed involved, and he is still President of his class 55 years later.

The Job Market
My first interview was at IBM. I thought I was going for an interview to become a trainee but they offered me a job as a secretary. One of the reasons I stayed with IBM is they allowed anybody who worked for IBM to put 10% of their salary into IBM stock. When I began my own business 10 years later, I funded it by selling my IBM stock, which had done very well.

Many of the women of the class of 1964 began their careers as secretaries. Then they looked for other jobs, but it was very difficult to advance in a company when you started as a secretary. IBM offered me a position in personnel after I had been there a few years, but I declined.

16

"You don't want me in personnel. When someone comes in and whines to me, I'll tell them to get on with it."

Our first child, Roger (Amherst '90) was born in 1968 and because of the generous benefits IBM offered, the total hospital bill was $2.76, and that was for the TV rental. I stayed home and started writing articles for the local Westchester magazine. I had my second child, Sandy (Penn '92) in 1970.

Entrepreneurship
When I put Sandy in elementary school in 1975, I needed to work in a job where I could have my own hours. Instead of returning to IBM, I decided to go into business for myself. I knew the garment business because of my mother. Another woman, talented and experienced in fabrics and textiles, joined me as my partner, and we started and ran "Whodunnit Fashions" for 12 years.

In the 1970s, every department store looked alike, carrying Anne Klein and Christian Dior apparel and accessories. We decided we could talk to new young designers and ask them to provide clothing in one color so that it would be exclusive to us. Our business would provide the "cream" to the department stores, allowing each to personalize their inventory. Ours grew to be an extremely successful organization, but the fashion business required extensive travel. I could no longer travel as much as I had done when my children were younger, so I sold the business to my partner.

My "Give Back" to Penn
I made the decision to become involved at Penn. I was never asked; women weren't. I worked my 20th Reunion, but really became involved

with my 25th. The men in the class of 1964 were so prominent I was afraid that none of the women would want to attend. So we made a highly organized effort to seek them out; they came and had a wonderful time.

Judy (second from right) with husband Howard and President Ford and Mrs. Ford in Vail, Colo.

In 1987, Al Shoemaker, chairman of the Board of

Trustees, had an idea to form a group of alumni women who would be supporters of other women's groups on campus. What he didn't realize was, when you put all these successful women together, they would develop their own agenda.

Our objective broadly was to raise the consciousness of the University family about the role of women at Penn and to provide a forum for the women on the campus — professors and students — to provide a place where they could be heard. Carol Einiger was the first chairperson, I was the second.

The Trustees' Council of Penn Women (TCPW) began as a networking organization and to provide mentoring and opportunity for women on campus in every way, shape and form. We offered the women on campus opportunities to network with other women.

Our council also was tasked with finding women who had not stayed in touch with the University. No one had ever kept track of these women. We found them, involved them in their class reunions and connected them with Penn again. Women graduates started giving money to Penn, although the Council had not started as a fundraising organization. We worked to create a culture where women understood if they want to be treated as valued alumnae, they had to give money, as the men do, to support their University.

Our culture shift created the incentive for women to get re-connected with Penn and also to identify the women who would become the next generation of leadership at Penn. That's exactly what happened. It's not a shock we had the first woman president of an Ivy League institution, Judith Rodin. That's all part of the culture change. This year we celebrated the 30th anniversary of the TCPW.

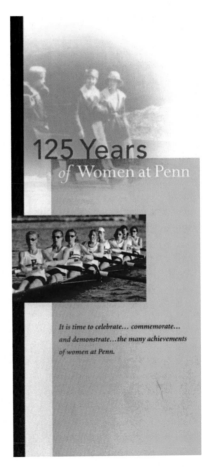

125 Years
of Women at Penn

It is time to celebrate... commemorate... and demonstrate...the many achievements of women at Penn.

The members of the Council fund the Council, and also funded the 125th Anniversary of Women at Penn (2001), which I was proud to chair. The 125th Anniversary brought over 1,000 women back to Penn for a celebratory weekend. We also created a book, *Franklin's Daughters*, which acknowledged our earlier graduates. Although women did not receive degrees until the early 1950s, they were allowed to take classes earlier. I believe it was the Quaker ethic that helped Penn understand women should not be discriminated against, and so it admitted them in 1876. (Accepting women — acknowledging that women could be worthy of an education — was a big leap of faith on Penn's part.)

The Trustees' Council of Penn Women was groundbreaking. Many women who worked on the 125th Anniversary of Women became Board of Overseer members and quite a few are now on the Board of Trustees. When I joined the board, there were very few women. At the 125th Anniversary of Women at Penn, Al Shoemaker said to me, "You started something that will reverberate at Penn for many years. We all owe you our thanks."

Volunteering, Not Retiring

Penn gave us confidence and the opportunity to do whatever we wanted in this extraordinary time. I don't think it's any surprise that both my husband Howard and I stayed active for so many years. We each were thrilled to receive Penn's Alumni Award of Merit.

My science background stood me in very good stead when I went on the board at Penn. The board needed someone with a science background to go on the University of Pennsylvania Hospital Board, and they asked me. When one of Penn's trustees became the President of Rockefeller University, a major scientific institute in New York, he recruited me to that board.

My Education degree prepared me to engage with the Center for Educational Innovation, a non-profit that provides inner-city schools with the additional support they need to become good schools. Being a history major was the catalyst for my membership on the New York Historical Society board. The oldest museum in Manhattan, it had been failing, and I was asked by the people responsible for its rebirth to come on board. Studying science, education, and history made my life much fuller and led to opportunities.

Women Today

My experience is no longer relevant in the way it was 20 years ago. Female students see a different world now. They're starting from a different point. We had no starting point. Everything we did, we created. But young women today don't see our experience as relevant to them because they don't have to start from scratch. Soon the glass ceiling is not going to exist when women become the heads of corporations in a greater number. It's going to shift; it's not going to stay the same. It's not going to be static.

Reflections

• The immigrant women or those like my mother who lived through the Depression years were determined their children would succeed. To me, they are the real heroes. My only mentor was my mother. She

was gutsy. She had great common sense and was a determined woman. That is basically what a woman needs for her success if she wants to raise a family and also run a business.

• I don't think you can accomplish everything you want to do without a supportive husband or partner. You need to have someone who understands you are going to be miserable if you don't follow your dream.

• I think any woman who started a career when I did — in the mid-1960s — feels she should have given more time to her family. Maybe deep down inside there is a nagging feeling, but I know if I didn't have my business, I might have been too overbearing with my children.

Judy and Howard at the White House for the 50th anniversary of the State of Israel.

• I was lucky to be born in a time when I had the opportunity to do what made me happy, and my kids have done just fine. They are independent and very happy. That's important.

• At the time we went to Penn, it was all brand new, groundbreaking, and we were very lucky to be at a place where you could take advantage of so many different leadership opportunities. I was president of my sorority. That doesn't sound like much, but it actually was.

• Everything is connected. My Penn experience led to business and board memberships and those led back to Penn.

None of the women portrayed in this book had any experience in doing what they did. We managed through perseverance and determination to succeed. We are proud of the contributions we have made to society.

REVEREND DR. BETTY BLOUNT

NURSE, TEACHER AND MINISTER

It's really God I credit with my success. I didn't understand that before, but I know now He was with me all the time, and He's with me now. I'll be 90 in 2017. When I go before Him, I want to tell Him what I have done. So with the time I have left, I want to write a full book of all my experiences. I don't have time to waste.

Reverend Dr. Betty Martin-Blount

My Early Years

From the time I was five years old, I knew I wanted to be a nurse. My mother and my maternal grandmother always encouraged me. They built up my self-esteem and self-worth.

Life was a continuing challenge for me as a woman of color. I graduated from the William Penn High School for Girls in Philadelphia, in the academic-Latin curriculum. At the time I was a student, the school would try to move girls off the academic track. They told the girls, "If you enroll in the achievement curriculum, you would still get your diploma at graduation." I went home, and I told my mother and my grandmother. My mother said, "No. You just stay right there."

Then my mother said, "I want you to take typing, because when you get in nursing school, you can type up your lessons." So I took typing as an elective. When I went into that class, the teacher said, "Now you colored girls, you're just wasting your time here, because no one will ever hire a colored girl to be a secretary." I told my mother.

I was so surprised to see my mother at the school the next morning. I don't know what happened, but the administrator called me up to the office, took me out of my typing class and assigned me to help in the nursery as my elective. I don't know where those children came from — maybe they were faculty children — I didn't think too much about it. I loved my work in the nursery.

Just before graduation, the school told me I had been chosen to write a graduation speech, but a Caucasian girl would read it. I was upset and told my mother. The next morning, again to my surprise, my mother went to the school. I don't know what she said, but one of the administrators called me into the office, and said "Betty, you can write your own speech, and you will be able to read it."

My mother worked on my speech, along with my aunt who also was a school teacher. When I went to the English teacher with my speech, she read it silently. She didn't say anything; she just gave me a yellow tablet and a pencil. She said in a very gentle voice, "Now Betty, why don't you write another speech?" I don't know if the speech was too polished for a high school senior or if the subject was not right for graduation. I sat right there in a chair beside her desk and wrote another speech, "The Common Man Emerges." My teacher liked the speech, and I delivered it at graduation. The graduation program listed me as the writer and the presenter. I also played the classical music accompaniment on the piano, but I received no recognition in the graduation program. That's the way it was.

I learned to play the piano because my mother paid 25 cents a week for my lessons. None of my siblings took the piano too seriously. When I came home from school, I had a snack, did my homework, and read; I loved to read. Then it was time for piano practice. By 8 o'clock I was in bed.

On Saturday mornings, I would turn on the radio to hear a program featuring a piano quartet, then pretend I was conducting. I could read and play any music. In my high school yearbook, a note under my name describes me as "a nimble-fingered pianist."

After high school graduation, the only place a black girl could go to nursing school in Philadelphia was Mercy Douglas, but it had a five-year waiting list. Since we had a lot of family in New York (I was born in Brooklyn and raised there before we moved to Philadelphia), my parents urged me to apply to Lincoln School for Nurses and Harlem Hospital. Lincoln School for Nurses admitted me.

The Beginning of the Dream
Lincoln was set up to support poor Negro girls and poor Jewish interns. It was a wonderful experience. The School watched us like hawks, and they taught us what to do and what not to do. And they built up our self-esteem. They said, "When you graduate from here, you'll be able to run any ward." (In those days, patient areas were called wards.) At the Lincoln graduation, I was listed as the piano accompanist. That was a special recognition. After I graduated from

As a senior nursing student.

22

Lincoln, I worked there for a short time, married a man from Brooklyn Law School, had a daughter and moved back to Philadelphia, living with my parents. Later, I became separated, then divorced. In Philadelphia, I learned Negro nurses could work only at night. It was difficult. So I signed up to do private duty nursing.

At graduation from Lincoln School for Nurses.

I went to the University of Pennsylvania Hospital. On a night shift, I was sitting in the room with my patient, and I remember many people coming and looking in the room. A cleaning lady said, "We heard the supervisor telling the family that you were the only person they could get, and people just wanted to see what you looked like." When I went to sign out, I saw on the printed sign out sheet, in all red capital letters. "ONE NITE ONLY — COLORED — NO RNs AVAILABLE." I said to myself, "I'm not going to do this." I changed direction and went into public health.

When I worked in public health, I wanted to advance to a higher level and knew a Bachelor's Degree in Nursing was required. The Philadelphia Department of Health sent me to Penn as a special student RN (Registered Nurse) with 30 credits. The first course I took was in English Composition. I received an A! That A made me feel so good. As the only minority woman in my class, I was forced to be a loner, but it didn't bother me; I had my life, going to class and enjoying everything. I especially loved Shakespeare.

After my 1964 graduation, I applied for the Master's program and was accepted. This was a new experience for me. There were only 13 of us in the Master's program. We had seminars and small group classes. Life was very different then for a woman of color. But thanks to President Kennedy and his administration, we had our tuition paid. We also received books and stipends.

I specialized in mental health and psychiatric nursing. The faculty met with us individually every week to evaluate us. I'll never forget one of the professors who used to say, "Betty is a born teacher." I enjoyed

23

teaching others. I wrote my Master's thesis about "A Study of Childhood and Adulthood Memories Consciously Recalled by Non-Psychotic and Psychotic Adults." One of the findings was that psychotic patients remembered frightening things that happened to them as children, when no one familiar to them was present to help. I recommended that immunizations should be given in a doctor's office or a community health clinic. Eventually, the schools no longer had "strangers" immunize children when they entered school. I received my Master of Science in Nursing degree in 1967.

Building Life-Long Relationships
During my Master's program, we had study groups and the students bonded. I met Betty Fallon, a Caucasian woman who became a life-long friend. Our children grew up together; we spent a lot of time together. After we graduated, both of us also established private practices. Betty Fallon taught me about having "to-do" lists, and I use them to this day.

I also met Delores Lake-Taylor in graduate school. She, too, is a life-long friend. For the past 30 years, Dee and I have been traveling buddies. We studied genealogy and, in 1993, we went to Henderson, North Carolina to research my family. We found the church, Flat Creek Baptist Church, where my grandparents were married. I also discovered my mother graduated from the Normal school. She was assigned to be a teacher, but she went to New York on a visit and never came back.

I was a city kid, while Dee was a country girl. She showed me so many things—even showing me how corn grows. Once on a trip to Arizona, I was mistaken for a Native American. People asked if they could take photos with me. People had preconceived notions of what people looked like, and I guess I looked Native American.

My Career Continues
At Penn, I was the only African-American woman in my class. To make my way in my career, I became a volunteer. I wanted to find out more about working with people who were bereaved. I volunteered at the Philadelphia Medical Examiners Office. Because I did so much volunteer work there, I received my certificate as a bereavement counselor.

In 1977, I entered Columbia University and received a Master's Degree in Education, with a concentration in Curriculum and Instruction and a minor in Mental Health and Psychiatric Nursing. In 1978, I received a Doctorate in Education (Ed.D), also from Columbia, in Curriculum and Instruction.

When I was in the doctoral program at Columbia, there were so many students, ministers, psychologists, sociologists and nurses that the

University hardly had enough patients for our clinical studies. I asked my professors if I could find my own experience. They said, "Sure."

I called Hahnemann Hospital in Philadelphia and asked about their community mental health centers. I met the woman who was the head of the catchment area, and she took me on. She talked to my professors and together they decided how she would evaluate me. And the experience I had was unbelievable, because I was able to do everything. Through my association with Hahnemann University Hospital, I also worked as a part-time mental health consultant and family therapist in an obesity clinic for children.

When it was time for me to end my clinical studies and receive my doctorate, I went to see my advisor to let her know. She said, "Well, did you set up a termination appointment with each client?" I said, "No." She said "Never abandon your clients. You have to set up an appointment with all of your clients and tell them." That was a life lesson.

My Joint Nursing/ Teaching Career

While I was receiving my Master's Degree from Penn, I worked at the Institute of the Pennsylvania Hospital. I was told the job as a Psychiatric Nursing Instructor would last for only one year. My supervisor and students from many different nursing schools evaluated me; mixed reviews were expected. This was another great experience, because I was the only person of color on the faculty and in the student body. The Director of the Affiliate Nursing Program gave me an excellent recommendation.

I applied to the Community College of Philadelphia and became an Assistant Professor. I didn't have my doctorate at that time, only the Master's Degree from Penn. I taught psychiatric nursing and the fundamentals of nursing to students who were studying to receive an Associate Degree in Nursing.

While I was at the Community College of Philadelphia, the head of the nursing program joined the National League for Nursing (NLN). When she later left to study for her doctorate degree, she recommended me. I got her job as a consultant in the NLN. That was another really good experience, but not without its challenges. When I would go out as a member of an NLN team, we were well-treated. When I went individually as a consultant, many times the person meeting me hadn't gotten the message I was African-American. When I would get off the plane, they'd be looking for someone other than me. It never even occurred to them "it's that woman over there." So I'd tell them what I would be wearing. Many times, when I would arrive at a school, we would waste two or three hours for people to come by and look. But after that, it was okay, because I really knew my "stuff."

After I received my Doctorate Degree (EdD) in 1978, I returned to the Community College of Philadelphia as an Associate Professor of Nursing and Head of the Department of Nursing. During that time, I made some visits to Associate Degree nursing programs for NLN. One time, I found myself up in the mountains of West Virginia. Nobody met me. I had a terrible room in an isolated section of the motel. In fact, I had brought my own food and I slept in my clothes. In the middle of the night, there was a sudden boom. The bed was shaking. A voice said, "This is the power of God and don't you ever forget it!" Boom. Boom. Boom. It was a frightening experience.

When I awoke in the morning, I went down to the lobby and saw all the people gathered together, scared to death. "Where were you?" "Somebody bombed the bank two blocks away." "The bomb blast shook the whole motel." Nobody ever thought to come get me. Outside the motel, it looked like another world war. Everything was devastated from that bomb. My experience was written about in the local newspaper. And I've never forgotten it, because then I knew I was filled with the power of God.

From CCP, I went to the Community College of Baltimore. They gave me a full professorship and named me Chairperson of the Department of Nursing. CCB was almost like a joke in Baltimore; the graduates couldn't pass their state boards; it was just a mess.

The first thing I did was to call in the people I had used in Philadelphia to work on the student's self-esteem. Then, I instituted a two-way program with the mental health practical nurses program. With the changes I made, the students of CCB got the highest state board tests of any school in Maryland, including Johns Hopkins, all the baccalaureate programs and all the diploma programs. The mayor of Baltimore proclaimed Nov. 4 of that year Community College of Baltimore Nursing Graduates Day.

From Baltimore, I went to Fort Hays State University in Hays, Kansas. I wanted to gain some experience with a baccalaureate program. They hired me because my previous employers vouched for me. Hays was an experience within itself, because the town is so small. The funniest story I can tell about Hays is one morning, as I was stepping out of the building where I lived, I saw something, I flew back into the apartment, called the administrative office and asked, "Will somebody come and get me?" One nurse arrived. She said, "Betty, that's a bunny rabbit." What did a city kid know?!!

The students from Hays had never been outside of their town and had no intentions of doing so. They were from wealthy families, but then their families had financial problems when the oil industry had fallen on hard times. Many of the students and their mothers had been abused. So, I had to introduce them to other ways of living without them feeling unsafe. The students didn't have to worry about state boards, because they passed those boards when they were sophomores. I had only seven students. I drove in the boondocks and gave the students different clinical experiences so they would get to know life outside of Hays. They loved it. It was a good experience for the students and for me.

Hays University offered me tenure but I thought I'd better go back to city life. I went to Richmond Community Hospital in Virginia and worked as a psychiatric staff nurse. Needing a breather, I enjoyed Richmond very much. The patients in Richmond were sick, really sick. While I was there, they established an award for the Nurse of the Year, and I received that award. When I was in Richmond, I also taught briefly at Rutledge Junior College.

My Return to Philadelphia is Interrupted Briefly

I returned to Philadelphia and worked part-time as a nurse. I thought I had finally retired in 1992 when a woman I met in Baltimore called me. She now was the president of a state community college in East St. Louis. She said, "Betty, I talked to the board; you've got to come, just for one semester. If we don't get an 80% passing rate, that's the end of nursing in this school." I told them you're the best in the country.

I said, "Well, I'll come one semester; because I recently remarried (in 1989) and I'm retired now." I didn't know it was "mission impossible." It was one of the worst, poorest areas of St. Louis. She gave me a full budget. I advertised. Nobody answered the ad. Finally somebody tipped me off. "You know, Dr. Blount, others are getting all your phone calls." I told the president about that. No one knew I had a room in the president's apartment in town, so she put in a private line. Calls were coming in, but when the people came and walked through those streets of East St. Louis, they flew out of there. They didn't want any part of it. Finally, a nun came. She was highly qualified, and we hired her. She was delighted, because the nuns lived within walking distance, the salary was good, and she could have her salary for her own purposes.

In the meantime, I had to work on getting the students to pass their exam. I used all the skills I learned in Philadelphia. I brought in

27

psychologists to work with the students. I talked with them about self-esteem. The nursing tests at that time were based on process, not the academics of the nursing program. We taught the students how to use the University computers. In the end, all but one student passed the nursing exam.

The philosophy of community education is that the best professors are the ones who stay in practice, and I knew that. Throughout my career, I never stopped volunteering. I volunteered at Evergreen, a psychiatric facility in Philadelphia. Then I worked part-time in private practice. Most of my private patients came from Evergreen. All of my volunteering helped me when I went to take my first certification test. I became board certified as a clinical nurse specialist in 1988. I maintained that certification until 2011 when I retired from private practice.

Despite being an African-American woman, I did not have any problem progressing through the ranks of any of the schools, or anyone making it difficult for me. *But I had to keep proving myself.*

The Personal Side of My Story
My daddy was a very wise man, because he left all the education and direction to my mother and my maternal grandmother. He gave us an allowance. I think it was 10 cents a week. I got my sisters to go on strike with me so he would raise it, and he gave us more. In 1945, 1946 and 1947, I spent my allowance on a radio show, The Voice of Prophecy, which offered a correspondence course. I just studied and loved it.

Many years later, I studied at a nearby church. My husband and I took classes together. I became ordained in 2001. I had no intentions of becoming a minister; I just wanted to learn. Then, I said to my daughter, "You know Theresa, I'm learning so much, I wish there was someplace that we could just learn more about the Bible…if we could only find a school." She called me and said, "I found one. It's in West Philadelphia, and they have Saturday classes." We registered, and I got in the curriculum. This was in 2009.

At the Baptist church I was attending in Philadelphia, I played the piano. The minister's wife said, "Betty, did you ever think about giving piano lessons?" I replied, "Well, I've never given anybody lessons, and really I'm not a piano teacher. But I could give children the beginning books." We agreed I would give the children beginner's books and take them as far as I was comfortable. Therefore, in April 2010, I started giving piano lessons at Antioch Baptist Church.

I developed the format for the children to play the piano for Sunday School. I simplified the music and explained to the head of the Sunday School this would be music everyone could sing. It was lovely. Meanwhile, I made arrangements with the Settlement Music School. The school agreed to accept the students. Later, the children had their first recital, and that was really something. I was thrilled.

Betty (second from left) with granddaughter Crystal, daughter Teresa Odom and grandson Ray Odom.

I truly believe the statement that before they are born, God has a plan and purpose for every child's life. Every child is important to God; he created every child as a unique individual with personality, gifts and talents different from all other children. Every child has the potential to be a star, because every child is a precious creation of God.

Retirement? Not Really

I continued to have a private psychiatric practice until 2011 when my husband became ill. We gave up everything and moved to New Jersey where we could get more help. Until then, we had maintained a residence at a senior facility in Center City Philadelphia.

Since I've retired, I still keep myself quite busy. I could sit home and be stiff and achy or get on out. I prefer to go out. I go to the senior center and relax. I've had all that Dr. Blount stuff. I want some peace. I just want to be Betty Blount.

CAMILLE BRADFORD, ESQ.

ATTORNEY AND HISTORICAL CONSERVATOR

I appreciate having the opportunity to share my recollections of Penn and to discuss the impact of my undergraduate education upon my career as an attorney.

In my own case I have derived the greatest satisfaction from my legal work and my other endeavors over the years that have, in some way, helped others and the causes in which I believe.

Camille Quarrier Bradford

Perspective
I understand one of the objectives of this project is to be a portrayal of various career obstacles women in our Class of 1964 have dealt with over the years. I didn't enter law school until 1974. By that time, the impact of the women's movement in the early 1970s had opened more doors than in 1964. Although obstacles and gender discrimination remained, the women's movement had made a difference. My law school class was about 20% women, a number of whom, like me, were returning to school after years out of college. The percentage of women enrolled in law schools grew over a number of years to become roughly equal with that of men. In 2016, the American Bar Association reported that women were now in the majority.

My Early Years
I grew up in Shawnee Mission, Kansas, and Bayside, New York, where I graduated from Bayside High School. Penn was my first choice among colleges, and I was thrilled when the acceptance letter arrived. I had wanted to go to a large Eastern university. I loved my years at Penn, the diversity of courses available, the University's many distinguished faculty members and the critical thinking they inspired.

In 1974, I was working happily on Wall Street in a position I enjoyed in the corporate finance department of a brokerage firm. Then my position was eliminated as part of the process of merging with a larger firm with its own corporate finance department. What next for me?

I had already passed the Registered Representative exam and considered working in another firm as a broker. However, I realized it would take a few years to build up a clientele to generate a reasonable income. That prompted me to consider law school, which would entail a comparable period of time. I entered law school in 1974 with an interest in securities law and with the goal of returning to Wall Street as an attorney.

From Finance to the Legal Profession

I attended Delaware Law School in Wilmington, Del., which is part of Widener University. At the time, I was living in Princeton, N. J., and it was a long trip back and forth each day. However, I commuted on Amtrak and was usually able to get a lot of reading done on the train. After my first year I made the law review, the *Delaware Journal of Corporate Law*, and was Managing Editor my last year. I also was one of the winners in the intramural moot court competition in my second year and served on the Moot Court Honor Society board in my last year. During the summer between my second and third years, I worked for the American Law Institute in Philadelphia writing summaries of court decisions for one of its publications.

Although I remained interested in securities law and hoped to return to Wall Street, one of my professors encouraged me to apply for a judicial

With Judge Halpern at reunion of his former law clerks, 1982. I am the only woman.

clerkship in New Jersey. I did so and was very fortunate to be offered a position as the law clerk for Judge Joseph Halpern of the Superior Court of New Jersey, Appellate Division. It was his next-to-last year before retirement from a long career as a judge, and I broke a glass ceiling of sorts as the first woman he had hired to be his law clerk.

After my clerkship was over, I joined a large law firm in New Jersey and worked on a variety of cases — primarily corporate, divorces, and estates. I left there about a year and a half later to join a small firm where Judge Halpern had become Of Counsel after his retirement from the bench. It was a wonderful experience to be able to work with him again and to seek his advice on various issues that arose in the cases I was handling. My experience there was centered around construction litigation, corporate, commercial transactions and divorce cases.

In 1984, a job change for my husband took us to Kansas. I worked as an in-house attorney for Kansas Power and Light Company in Topeka, handling construction litigation, contracts, environmental and a variety of general corporate matters.

Another job change for my husband resulted in a move to Denver in 1990. I continued to do legal work, primarily for my former boss in New Jersey who had established a solo practice. Initially I was commuting back and forth from Denver to New Jersey every week for a year. Later I acted as local counsel for construction cases he had pending in several courts in Colorado.

Despite the commuting back and forth, I enjoyed that time very much. It was good to be able to concentrate on work during the week and enjoy the weekends in another part of the country.

Preserving the Legacy of My Stepfather
The decade of the '90s also was a time of transformation. Like many other attorneys, my interests shifted to other pursuits. I also moved my mother from the East Coast to Denver and enjoyed having the opportunity to be with her more. She had been the Chair of the Docents at the New Jersey Governor's mansion and, upon moving to Denver, became a docent at the Colorado Governor's mansion. She continued to do that until age 93!

I also became interested in preserving the legacy of my stepfather, Dr. Howard R. Driggs. In addition to his career as an English professor and department chair in the New York University School of Education, he became well-known as a western historian and was the author of over 50 books in both fields. He also was the president of the Oregon Trail Memorial Association and its successor, the American Pioneer Trails Association. The mission of these organizations was preservation of the trails over which the pioneers emigrated to the west in the 1800s and which were used by the Pony Express. My stepfather's works included *The Pony Express Goes Through* (1935), *Westward America* (1942) and *The Old West Speaks* (1956). The Howard R. Driggs Elementary School in Holladay, Utah, is named in his honor.

My stepfather's papers are now archived in the Special Collections Library at Southern Utah University, where his career as an educator began. I am on the Board of Friends of the Sherratt Library and edit its newsletter. In 2009, I established an annual lecture series at the university in honor of my stepfather.

I am active in the Oregon-California Trails Association, which has carried on the mission of the organizations my stepfather headed. I am a past board member and am President of the Colorado chapter. Presently, I serve on several committees of the national organization, including the

Governance Committee of which I am Chair, and the Investment
Committee, which utilize both my investment and legal experience.

**Speaking at "Trails to the Shining Mountains," a 2015 joint symposium of
the Rocky Mountain Map Society and the Oregon-California Trails
Association.**

I also have been invited to give presentations on my stepfather's work to
various historical groups in the West, which I enjoy immensely. In 2010, I
gave a presentation at the National Postal Museum in Washington, D.C.,
in connection with the observance of the 150th anniversary of the Pony
Express.

Looking Back and Advice to the Students Today
I am very grateful for the opportunities Penn created for me after
graduation and for the lifelong friendships I made there. I presently
serve on the board of the Penn Alumni Club in Denver. I enjoy both this
ongoing connection with the University and the opportunity to meet
alumni from other classes now living in Colorado.

I also am very grateful for the influence my mother had upon my life.
She was a wonderful role model. She graduated from the University of
Kansas in 1930 and worked first as a reporter for the *Kansas City Star* at a
time when such opportunities for women were limited. She inspired me
to take an interest in writing at an early age. When it came time to choose
a major at Penn, I chose the English Department, which offered a
number of journalism courses and the option to choose that as a
concentration. I had excellent professors and enjoyed the "real life"
experiences in reporting they incorporated into class discussions. In 2000
I took Mother to her 70th reunion at KU. She was the only one from her
class there. Although that was sad, the rest of the weekend was a
wonderful walk down memory lane for her, and she did it all without a
golf cart! I hope to be able to do that in 2034.

Although Penn was the link between my teenage years and adulthood, entering law school 10 years later was more of a transformative experience. In addition to the great sense of relief law school was over, I recall vividly the great sense of optimism I felt at the graduation dinner about the future and the opportunities open to me to "do good" in the world with a law degree.

Practicing law brings many high moments of satisfaction, but day-to-day life in a law firm also encompasses much mind-numbing work, long hours, billing pressures and other stressful demands. Many surveys of satisfaction reveal a startling lack of it among attorneys, sometimes driven by a disturbing lack of civility among adversaries.

Nevertheless, I feel strongly that obtaining a law degree and practicing law for at least some period of time is one of the most valuable life experiences one can have. For those who choose to move on to other pursuits, there are many opportunities in business, government and other fields where a legal background can be well-utilized.

With Michael Benson, former President of Southern Utah University, at a reception in May 2008 in connection with the opening of the Howard R. Driggs Room in the Special Collections Library, in honor of my stepfather.

RONA COHEN

DREAMS OF A CHEMISTRY CAREER FADE AS ONE ACADEMIC CLASS SPARKS A CAREER IN TECHNOLOGY

Being born in the mid 20th century provided my generation with a climate of great opportunity, but we also faced many cultural blockades as women. I overcame these challenges through three overriding personality traits that have driven my path through my lifetime. They are curiosity, risk taking, and climbing over or through walls. Even today, I continue to pursue personal and business challenges.

Rona Solomon Cohen

My Early Years

My parents owned a pharmacy and home in Crescentville, a row house community in Northeast Philadelphia. I attended Olney High School in Philadelphia. I loved the challenge of being competitive as a student and graduated third in my class. I won a Board of Education partial scholarship to Penn and also received a Pennsylvania Senatorial scholarship. My parents supported me with the rest of the tuition to attend the University of Pennsylvania. I started as a commuter and begged my parents to let me live on campus. I moved into the Women's Residence Hall in its earliest years.

As the scientist in the family, I won a science award in eighth grade and then a variety of science awards in high school. In my senior year of high school, I hosted a Sunday morning program on public television with the Franklin Institute called, "Why in the World." One summer, I also had an opportunity to go to Central High School in Philadelphia to build a radio. I was the only girl in the otherwise all male group at Central.

My parents believed a woman was supposed to get married and pursue a study program where she would have a career as a backup financially, such as nurse, teacher or librarian. My father was a pharmacist, and he wanted me to go to Penn. My father did not have a son and he focused a lot of his unfulfilled wishes on me, a willing receiver. My mother felt if Temple University was good enough for my sister and my father, it certainly was good enough for me.

I was accepted at Penn, and thought my future would be in medicine because my male cousin went to medical school. My dad had also wanted to be a physician, but was unable to finance it as it was during the Depression. My parents thought medicine was a bad idea. At Penn, I studied philosophy, and I wanted to be a philosophy major. My father put his foot down and said, "No. How can you make a living as a philosopher?" So I decided to major in chemistry.

Life at Penn

It appeared to me the women at Penn were smarter than the men because of the admissions process at the time. Since there were far fewer women than men, it was much more competitive for women. Every time you were in a large class, you just knew the women were smarter than the men.

When I got to college, I didn't feel limited until I hit several walls. I felt lost the first year. And I knew medical school would be difficult for me to apply to without my parents' backing. The women in our class who went on to medical school were special. About 20 percent of the women who majored in chemistry were nursing students.

I did well in organic chemistry. Unfortunately, I was unaware of the requirements to obtain a Bachelor of Science degree in Chemistry. So it came as a surprise in my senior year to learn that if I wanted a B.S., I would have to add several semesters of additional courses. It was explained to me that since I was in the College for Women, there were a large number of liberal arts courses required for graduation. Hence, the curriculum left little opportunity to take the necessary courses for a Bachelor of Science in Chemistry and still graduate in four years. I ultimately received a Bachelor of Arts degree in Chemistry. Madeleine M. Joullié, the first woman to join the Penn's chemistry faculty, was my advisor. She was a role model.

My first experience with applied mathematics was in my senior year. I needed another credit. A couple of my friends who were math-oriented said, "Why don't you take EE523, an electrical engineering course? It's interesting; it's numbers theory. You'll like it." This class was being offered because the first commercial computer, ENIAC, had been developed at Penn. The class focused on computation and using basic machine language to write programs. I took that class at night, not realizing how valuable this class would become in my career.

I found the professors in the math department very condescending. They didn't want women in their classes unless they were going into math education, so they treated women differently. I liked math but it was never going to be my future. Professors never discussed entrepreneurial careers or leadership.

One of the drivers for me to be successful was my desire to afford everything life had to offer. But I really could not see my career as being in chemistry. Rohm and Haas and Pennwalt (Philadelphia-based chemical companies that recruited on campus) told me there were no roles for me in chemistry because I was too educated to be a lab technician, and they could not have any males working for a female, so I couldn't run anything.

Other aspects of my Penn experience did enrich my later business life and my "other" life, particularly my later-in-life pleasures. I took Russian history and music. I also loved philosophy and took seven philosophy courses. I really enjoyed ethics and other philosophical subjects. Those classes have stayed with me through my life.

Another "wall" I encountered was the pressure my classmates and I felt to find a mate and at least get engaged before we graduated. At the time, marriage was considered the only path for women to a secure and culturally acceptable future. And in fact, in my sophomore year, I was introduced to the man who would become my husband for 46 years. His name was Arnold B. Cohen, and he was graduating from the Penn Law School the month after we met. Since we were going to be living near each other in the Philadelphia suburbs that summer, he phoned me and we started to date.

Our romance continued and we got engaged in 1964 after my graduation. We married in December of 1964. Due to his interest in teaching law, Arnie applied for and received a teaching position at the Bolt Law School of the University of California at Berkeley. I got a job, through a campus interview, at Shell Oil Company in Emeryville, Calif. We travelled out West to our new jobs in his MGB sports car with a suitcase apiece.

While my husband was teaching at Bolt, my first job at Shell was as a chemical abstractor in the Information/Library Department. We abstracted and indexed internal publications Shell scientists produced monthly, worldwide. My job was to read in-house reports in my area of expertise, polypropylene extrusion through pipes. I spent a year coding and indexing all written material by researchers on bubbles in pipes. It was tedious and uninspiring.

Even though we found the Bay area to be fascinating, Arnie and I decided our future was back East with our respective families.

My Career as a Software Programmer

When I returned to Philadelphia, one of my Penn female classmates, the one who had suggested the engineering class at Penn, recommended I go to an interview at General Electric. GE was looking for people who understood numerical analysis and calculus. I took the test and began a career in software development. GE surmised if I could work with large integral equations, I could learn how to program a computer. So GE trained me in software languages. It was a life-changing event for me. I didn't think so at the time, although "I took this job in the context of a bigger future." I also was driven by my curiosity in this world of mathematical modeling.

I worked on two large re-entry systems projects; one was for NASA's Voyager Lander. I became an expert in shockwave analysis, which involves the area around a space vehicle's exterior as it re-enters the earth's atmosphere. I spent three years developing software to analyze the data being recorded around the re-entry vehicle. That data then drove how the space engineers managed the vehicle itself. (Voyager Lander is now in the Smithsonian Air and Space Museum.)

I left GE when I became pregnant with twins. I found out about the twins just two weeks before they were born, and delivered them six weeks prematurely (there were no ultrasounds then). I survived the challenge and was fortunate to have two great daughters, Julia Beth and Jessica Lynne.

Knowing I was having two babies left me speechless. I left GE voluntarily and did not even inquire about their maternity leave policy. I also do not recall anyone coming back to work at GE after having a child. The only women who returned were those who had had miscarriages. This led to a population of females at that GE facility who were childless.

When the twins were about three months old, I took a part-time consulting position with Temple University and helped the faculty with their projects using FORTRAN, a computer programming language. I also taught FORTRAN. I got this job through a lead from a Penn classmate who was, at that time, working for Control Data Corporation (CDC), the company that had sold their computers to Temple University.

About three years later I had a third daughter, Alison Jane, and decided to be a stay-at-home mom for a while. I improved my tennis game and made several close friends who also were at home with small children. But fate and financial reality came into play when my husband decided to leave the practice of law and become a professor at Villanova Law School. I knew I was going to have to contribute financially to our household.

Through my Penn classmate, Susan Miller Hoffman, I was introduced to an opportunity at the Institute for Scientific Information in Philadelphia. The job description required an understanding of chemical nomenclature and experience in machine level coding languages. I had those skills and was hired, becoming the only female in an IT department of about 18 people. The twenty women chemists who did the abstracting were "heads down" workers, not risk-takers. I had a private cubicle, a phone and flexible work hours. The chemists had none of those privileges and worked in a highly regimented bull pen. They also were primarily graduates of the local all-female Catholic colleges. I could not have survived in their work environment.

Soon, I developed an overarching view of my career as being in the business of the business. Going forward, every job I took was in the business of the business in technology as opposed to technology that was only bookkeeping. A lot of women became experts in COBOL; these jobs were dead-ended. It was almost like a staff position with no advancement possibilities.

In every decision I made, my technology background created the product. At ISI, I developed software that actually took the data about the compounds the abstractors encoded, managed them, and created search algorithms. ISI sold subscriptions for all the database tapes to chemical and pharmaceutical companies worldwide.

Although my clients were located all over the world, I didn't get to see them. My boss went to install systems in Germany. He told me to my face I couldn't go because, "If he were my husband he wouldn't want to stay home with three young children." In the 1970s, I helped form the Network of Women in Computer Technology to focus on networking

and gender issues in the workplace. I became a Feminist. I did meet Betty Friedan while I was at Penn.

Childcare arrangements were always challenging, as there were not many options available. My husband and I traded places for this daily responsibility as he had a great deal of flexibility as a professor.

Daughters Alison, Jessica and Julie with Rona and Arnie.

My daughters were very active and curious children, and they did well in their early school years. They ultimately went on to play competitive sports and attend Ivy League colleges and graduate schools. Julia attended Harvard University, played varsity field hockey there and graduated *summa cum laude*. She worked on Wall Street, graduated from Harvard Business and Harvard Law Schools, worked for many years at McKinsey and ultimately became a partner at Korn Ferry, a consulting and executive search firm. Jessica attended Yale University, was captain of the lacrosse team, graduated from Harvard Medical School and is currently Chief Medical Officer at Partners Health, based in Boston. They each have three children. My third daughter, Alison, graduated from Penn, received an MBA degree from Harvard, obtained her CPA and CFA, and has had a career in Manhattan in financial services. She is currently a partner in a private investment management firm and lives in Brooklyn with her husband and two children.

I received my MBA in 1980 from Drexel University. ISI had said to me clearly, "Nice that you got your MBA, but it doesn't mean much here. Don't expect to get out of IT. You'll maintain these systems. Be happy. Be content. Just do your job." Do your job? I thought, "This isn't satisfying me," so I left ISI in the early 1980s to go to a computer timesharing company. I wanted to do something different—to get out into the marketplace. The timesharing business—SBC (the Service Bureau Company)—had been owned by IBM, but had been recently acquired by Control Data Corporation.

SBC interviewed 260 people for 13 positions that year, and I got a job with them. They wanted soldiers—people who were going to go out, follow their paradigm to sell and go out for the "kill." The people who were hired into that operation were unique people,

At the IBM training center in Tarrytown, N.Y.

mostly men coming out of the military. SBC was open to women; they hired beautiful women, and they hired women with extraordinary experience. I was offered a job as a systems marketing representative because I knew FORTRAN and Basic. SBC needed someone who understood the software. The man who interviewed me was ex-military.

He asked, "What do you think my golf score is?" I guessed his golf handicap, and he gave me the job. (Very strange interview!)

I had no idea what I was getting into, really none, but it was an amazing experience. SBC taught me planning paradigms, how to manage a business environment and how to manage a group.

That job changed my life again — it was a seminal experience and changed who I became in business.

SBC did a big "head job" on me. SBC taught you everything; you were molded. They had the business skills down to details I had never seen or heard before. I hadn't played team sports, so I didn't understand the concept of operating within a team as a way to win. SBC taught me how to win. I learned things that people don't learn anywhere else. It empowered me for the rest of my life.

SBC operated as an independent unit at CDC and still perceived itself as IBM. The IBM-derived sales training lasted for a year. Although I was a technical person, I supported the client and actually did what was called pre-sales marketing. I would create examples of how to use the software, or look at what the company was doing and advise them on what we could do for them. I ended up in a financial group working with the insurance industry, becoming an expert on both life insurance and property casualty insurance applications. Since this was a very legislatively-impacted arena, with laws changing all the time, the software had to keep up.

Another Job in a Different Field
After I received my MBA, I left the hands-on technology field because I wanted to use my MBA degree. I went to Auerbach Publishers, a publisher for IT professionals, as a product manager. Auerbach Publishers was acquired by a large Canadian global publishing company. This company eliminated the Auerbach marketing department, and I was out of a job. I looked for work in the Philadelphia market, but there was nothing which appealed to me.

New York City was really foreign to me but, at the time, I was a significant contributor to our personal financial picture. I just was motivated by the fact I

In Amsterdam while on a business trip for Auerbach.

41

needed to get something that was interesting, and I didn't think I could find that type of opportunity in Philadelphia. Against all odds, I took a job that involved commuting daily to New York City; everybody tried to talk me out of it. I ended up being employed by Dun & Bradstreet and commuting for three years to New York City from Philadelphia.

While I was at D&B, an opportunity came to me to start a branch in Philadelphia of a technical services company based in Buffalo, N.Y. I flew from Philly to Buffalo and interviewed with Computer Technology Group (CTG). I got the Philadelphia Branch Manager job and all went well. I worked with the chief technology officers at many of the large Philadelphia-based companies. I grew the operation and had 80 people working for me. It was a great experience.

After five years at CTG, I was recruited by Oracle in the early 1990s. A headhunter had called me about a position to manage a process industry consulting practice. I got a great job offer from Oracle which entailed being a national manager for a vertical-focused consulting practice. I was named the manager for the Oracle Consulting Group in their process industry vertical market, running a consulting sales and delivery organization for chemicals and pharmaceuticals nationwide.

We were going gung-ho. In fact, Oracle had a sales contest called the Gold Rush. We all were meeting in my office in Iselin, N.J., when a man came in dressed like a cowboy shooting guns—Gold Rush—and I got $20,000 that day because my group had been so successful. Two weeks later I got fired. Oracle unilaterally cut the entire Oracle Consulting Group. Larry Ellison wrote about this decision in his book.

Talent is not always valued. Business is not a democracy; it's just whatever works for the company at the time. I didn't know how to leverage off the Oracle experience, so I talked to a company in Philadelphia called Day & Zimmerman (D&Z), which had a subsidiary called Day Data Services.

I saw two futures that were big: one in document management and another in sales force automation. I was hired by D&Z as a Director of Marketing. Although D&Z did not put a lot of money into my department, we made it work and even initiated several new successful businesses.

Then, the D&Z chair decided he didn't want to carry Day Data anymore; he just closed it one day. I had all these great programs going on and said to myself, "Oh, my God, what do I do now?" I was 48 and since my options at D&Z were very limited, I left the company.

In my job search, yet again, I was offered an opportunity with a new technology company in the hand held and wireless industry. The unique company for which I worked was Poquet Computer Corporation, owned by Fujitsu and based in California. Their vision was to have a handheld computer that was mobile. (This was in 1994 when mobile devices were in their infancy.) I was selling hardware and applications for wireless communication. Most were being purchased by the military. My territory stretched from Virginia to Northern New Jersey. The operation folded after a year as Poquet could not deliver in a timely fashion on the form factor or wireless requirements to meet client needs.

My Entrepreneurial Career

I began my own company, Wellinger & Associates, Inc., and started the business in my lower level family room as world headquarters. I saw myself as a management consulting firm, but the real financial rewards came in recruiting talent for the hungry IT market.

I turned to all the people I knew in the vendor community, and they gave me opportunities and business. It was always on a contingent basis; hence, I had no salary, no vacation, no benefits, but it was an opportunity and the best time of my life. I had no one dictating policy to me.

But then, in 2009, my husband became sick. He had a challenging illness, and since my daughter was a doctor in Boston, we moved to Boston for my husband's treatments at the Dana-Farber Cancer Institute. I closed up our house in Philadelphia.

In Bath, England, while negotiating a very large business deal.

Three weeks after moving to Boston, my daughter Julia called to tell me about her friend who worked for a company called LivingSocial, based in Washington, D.C. They were trying to hire a lot of salespeople. Her friend asked my daughter, "Would your mom help us out?"

Living Social had workflow management software you had to use if you wanted to work remotely. They had no instruction menu, nobody to talk to, nothing...but as a software developer, I was very comfortable with technology, so I sat down and figured it out. I thought, "Well, I can do this."

They were going to send me 150 resumes a week. I created a profile, then I'd search for resumes matching that profile in the 150 they would send. As soon as I discovered the profile, I was flying. Although I don't know exactly how many individuals I interviewed, it was well over 2,000 people in the year and a half I did this. Six months into this work effort, Amazon invested 50 million dollars in the company.

It was challenging and, over time, I earned considerable compensation working part-time, anywhere I wanted to, and never meeting the candidates.

Widowhood, Retirement, then Un-Retirement

After I lost my husband, the hardest thing for me was getting out socially again. I met a man online who also was a recent a widower. He had been a medical professor at the Hospital of the University of Pennsylvania. Even though our direct paths had never crossed, we had many acquaintances in common. We have partnered together in a new business venture in the medical device arena and now have had three patents published and great acceptance of this new technology. We have been together for the past five years.

Surprisingly, I have never formally retired. I continued to stay active in my trade association and other tech organizations in Philadelphia. I also have served clients on a project basis over the past seven years, most of whom came through personal referrals.

In 2016, I was honored by the Network of Women in Computer Technology. I was the past president and had helped build the organization. This was very uplifting.

After you were a successful business woman, entering the world of the non-working female is really hard. You're walking into an environment where non-career women play by very different rules. You don't have the power behind you that you had when you were working. The world has different dimensions when you are retired and a widow. It's very hard to accept; it's humbling.

Career Success

My female cohort generation had no precedent to follow nor did we have mentors. My career success was based on a need to self-actualize, nurtured by curiosity and tenacity. Perhaps the Women of the Class of 1964 were ultimate self-actualizers in Maslow's Hierarchy of Needs. But we didn't think of ourselves as women, not even aware of anything like a glass ceiling.

SANDRA FISHER

WOMEN'S AND CIVIL RIGHTS ACTIVIST, FITNESS AND WELLNESS ENTREPRENEUR AND INTERNATIONAL TEACHER

Each of us makes decisions about our lives; hopefully, good ones. My best decisions come from following my intuition — does it feel right in my gut? Then, it's how you deal with the situations that count. I look for the silver lining and the opportunities — how can I make this situation more productive, satisfying, healthy and rewarding to others and myself?

I believe women benefit mightily from support of all kinds — from friends, family, business colleagues and associations, and psychotherapy. This works two ways — receive it thankfully and give it generously! Every woman should build her network and own personal advisory board of all ages to call on. Whether it's to look at her resume, solve a business or personal problem or whatever the situation demands, a personal advisory board is a plus.

Sandra Crawford Lotz Fisher

My Early Formative Years in New Jersey

I grew up in Kearny, N. J. to age twelve, surrounded by my mother's large Scottish family who had emigrated to the U.S. in 1912. When WWII started, my father enlisted in the U.S. Army. My mother and this six-month-old moved in with my grandparents. My mother had studied dietetics and nutrition at Pratt Institute. During the War my mother worked as a dietitian for Dupont in Kearny. After the War my mother, father, two-year-old brother and I moved three blocks away. My mother launched her catering business, while raising a growing family of four children, managing a household, being president of the Junior Women's Club and Hospital Auxiliary and becoming the first woman on the Board of West Hudson Hospital. My father worked as a sales manager and attended Rutgers Law School at night on the GI Bill. My independent streak began here.

I was expected to help my mother prepare and serve food, help with the younger children, and make intelligent decisions on my own. By ten years old, I rode my bike for miles, took the bus alone to Newark to shop and meet Grandma at work in Bamberger's, visited the dentist, and attended Mosque Theatre concerts with friends. My extended family provided an enormous safety and social net for my parents and for my growing up with such independence. My mother was a go-getter with unbounding energy and both my parents were salespeople, hard-workers, and attuned to taking advantage of opportunities. They laid the foundation for my approach to school, marriage, career, community and, indeed, life.

My world changed dramatically when we moved to Maplewood, N.J., a more upscale suburban community about 15 miles further west, which had an excellent education system. But it was made clear to me that parents in Maplewood didn't let *their* daughters be independent, walk home from the movies, or travel to Newark alone. Needless to say, these "new" norms created lots of inner and behavioral conflicts for me. I attended Columbia High School where 95% of the students went on to college, but the suburbs felt confining and I wanted an urban college.

When asked what I wanted to do when I grew up, my reply was to work in the Foreign Service. I had no idea what that really meant, but as someone fascinated by foreign cultures, religions and governments, this seemed rife with opportunities to go far away from the suburbs and explore the world.

Most students in my class applied to three colleges. Mine were Syracuse University (my dad graduated there in '31 and was very active with the Alumni Club of North Jersey), Pembroke College of Brown University, and Penn. I learned an important life lesson at my interview at Pembroke. The Admissions officer asked, "What's your feeling about coming to Pembroke?" With a sixteen-year-old's earnest honesty, I said, "It's great, but I really like Penn." Needless to say, I didn't get into Pembroke, but the take-away has served me well over the years — Never say "no" and close the door to a potential opportunity.

Wanting desperately to go to a city college, I visited my cousin who went to Penn Nursing School. Penn looked heavenly. I was thrilled when I was accepted. When my father dropped me off on the first day at the Penn Sherwood Hotel, a temporary dorm, I thought, *"I've found my people!"* Everyone in the dorm was interested in exploring opportunities and eager to learn, discuss, and get some neat dates!

Penn, My Sorority and My Exposure to Foreign Affairs
At Penn, my major was political science, but my courses took me on mind-expanding adventures. I had many terrific professors, including Dr. Alvin Rubinstein (Soviet Politics), Dr. Edward Janovik (Political

Science), Drs. Richard, Brilliant, David Robb, John McCoubrey, Malcomb Campbell (History of Art), and Dr. Mariner (Opera) stand out in my mind, but none ever inquired, nor did I expect to be asked, "What do you want to do with your life and how would you make that happen?"

An enormous influence was my sorority, Kappa Kappa Gamma, with its interesting, independent women from both public and private school backgrounds — the latter being a very different world from mine. The pluses of Kappa were fantastic. Kappa entertained professors for lunch, offered leadership opportunities, made budgets, participated in national conventions and worked with dedicated women alums. One Penn and Kappa alum who made a lasting impression as a role model was Ruth Branning Malloy, a photographer, poet, writer for national magazines, married woman and a mom. Mrs. Malloy lived across from the Kappa house on Locust Street and

Me with my Kappa Kamma Gamma sorority sister, Candace Bergen, in 1964.

frequently popped in to give her Serendipity Award, which recognized girls who contributed quietly to Kappa and Penn.

My sorority volunteered at Penn's foreign-student teas on Thursday afternoons and socialized with the foreign graduate students. I had lunch with the nephew of the prime minister of India (where else could this happen but Penn!), and became friends with an MBA from Mexico. We met again in Mexico City when I went on the Experiment in International Living to Mexico between my junior and senior year. Connections started early.

My sorority also nominated me for Homecoming Queen — Miss Campus Chest (really, and I won!) and a Kappa sister recommended me for a well-paying student's job at the Wharton School, which I needed for spending money. I also gained leadership experience being on the board of the Bennett Union (the women's student union), and athletic recognition being a soloist on the Pennguinettes synchronized swimming team.

Then, there was my red Vespa motor scooter. I decided to follow my gut, keep moving, and buy a scooter in June 1961. I was the only woman in Philadelphia to ride a scooter. It's hard to believe in 2018, but I stopped traffic, driving it down a busy highway to Philly without a helmet!

On my red Vespa in 1961.

One academic policy error Penn made (corrected years ago) allowed students in the College for Women to skip the math and lab science courses that were required for men in the College, and substitute psychology, geology and an "easier" version of economics. The message seemed to be that women had no need to stress taking the more difficult subjects unless their careers required them. I took geology rather than math and hated it. The math would have been helpful with my difficult statistics course, and lab science would have proved valuable when I took applied physiology in graduate school.

Penn offered the world. Students came from all over, and if you were interested in reaching out, Penn offered numerous vehicles to meet and develop relationships with interesting people.

I Met My Husband
Another person who greatly influenced me was Richard Fisher (C '64, MA '67). We met in my junior year, married a week after my graduation, and lived in Philadelphia until 1974 when we moved to New York City. Facebook CFO Sheryl Sandberg said in her book that one of the most important decisions a woman makes is the man she marries; that was very true in my case. Richard was an English major, Executive Editor of the *Daily Pennsylvanian*, and went on to work as a journalist, theatre critic and publisher of a small guidebook for business. We had planned to join the Peace Corps, but Richard's severe allergy to bees prevented that.

Richard opened up a whole other world for me because he came from a wealthy, Jewish, philanthropic real estate family in New York City, while I came from a middle class, gentile family in Maplewood. But our values were the same. Although we divorced after 14 years in 1978, we continued amicably to raise our children and consider us part of one another's families. My twenties — being married, establishing friendships and teaching, studying, having children and trying to change the world through activism — were an incredible period both in our country and for me personally.

Teaching Social Studies and World Cultures

In the fall of 1964 I substitute taught in Philadelphia schools, enrolled in Penn's Graduate School of Education, and studied Urban Education with Dr. Howard Mitchell. My goal was to teach secondary social studies in the city, but no jobs materialized. I typed 20 resumes and received an offer to teach American Social Problems and World Cultures from Lower Merion High School (LMHS), an excellent school on Philadelphia's suburban Main Line. It was a dream job. Lower Merion had free course credits from Penn in exchange for hosting student teachers; therefore, most of my graduate education was free. Social Studies is so broad a field that my course studies from 1965 through 1967 ranged from American Political Parties, Cultural Geography, History of China Post 1900, History of South Asia to 1200, and Criminology—an intellectual smorgasbord. I loved them. Although the salary was low, my husband and I both worked, which meant we could do more than if we had to live on one salary.

Community Activism and Keeping My Job When I Was Pregnant

In 1967 David Hornbeck, a community activist in education in Philadelphia, visited Lower Merion High School's principal, hoping to establish a connection between suburban teachers and the city. The principal said he had one teacher who would be interested—me—and that changed the direction of my life. I became in involved in the struggle for civil rights and women's rights.

I joined People for Human Rights and, with David's help, organized Project Start (Suburban Teachers Against Racism), composed of public and private school teachers in the Philadelphia suburbs. At LMHS, we organized the Committee for Understanding to bring black and white students together to explore racial issues and how we could work together. We arranged for Black speakers (the first ever to be in the school) to address these tumultuous issues.

When I was pregnant with my first child in 1969, the school district forbade women to stay in the classroom past five months. I wasn't going to sit home for four months, so I created an Independent Study Project for seniors (known to slack off before graduation), to do projects with professionals and the government—and the superintendent approved it. To my knowledge, this was the first project of its kind in a high school. The lesson for me is when I can't do one thing, create something I want to do and try to make it happen. Nothing ventured, nothing gained. In all, it was an honor to teach at LMHS.

The women's movement was just beginning in the early 1970s. I was a founder of the Women's Political Caucus in Philadelphia; organized the first women's conference in 1970 held at Penn's Christian Association; and demonstrated and advocated for reproductive rights for women. During this time, many women went through a process of rethinking their careers. Many teachers and social workers decided to become lawyers and doctors. I considered law school, but couldn't envision myself doing the analytic research and writing required. My gut screamed, "No!"

A benefit of my networking was that a History teacher on my Project START committee from Germantown Friends School offered me a half-time teaching position there after I had my first child — a perfect balance for my life. I taught at Germantown Friends School from 1970 to 1972, gave birth to my second child, worked in politics, ran as a McGovern delegate in 1972, and made plans to move to New York City.

Moving to New York City – Changing Careers – Divorcing

In 1974, my life changed when Richard decided to return to New York to work at Fisher Brothers, his family's real estate business. This was an incredibly difficult move for me. My life in Philadelphia was rich with friends, connections and work. In New York, Richard was gone from the house for 12 hours a day while I was at home with two little children. In Philadelphia, we had an "equal" marriage. In New York, our marriage fell apart. My challenge was to create a new life. To start, I made a business card, refusing to give little scraps of paper with my contact info to new acquaintances!

We separated in 1976 and divorced in 1978. After the split I did two life-changing Outward Bound courses, in North Carolina and the Cascades in Washington State. Fascinated with the mind-body connection, I enrolled in the Masters program in Applied Physiology at the Teachers College of Columbia University with a specific goal: to become the Director of Fitness and Health at the YWCA of NYC, an institution that reflected my values to eliminate racism. I started work there in 1978, and my parents came from New Jersey to watch the kids at night while I attended courses. I worked with women from ages 20 to 85, created and taught exercise classes for different ages and health conditions, introduced the emerging field of Aerobics, and networked with city agencies and non-profits. I increased my program's revenue by over 300% and was asked to write a book on my program. Management offered me a pittance and would not give me the credit I wanted, so I refused to write it. My glowing performance reviews changed to terrible that last year. That's when I decided to start my own business

Starting My Fitness and Wellness Business

In 1985 I founded Fitness by Fisher Inc., where I designed motivational and customized fitness, wellness and stress management programs for corporate and association meetings. I also wrote articles, did motivational speaking, created Fitness Breaks for training programs and made a tape, "Freeway Flex: Stretch and Tone Exercises to Do While U Drive." My always-salesman father helped me enormously by planning sales calls, and I landed some large pharmaceutical and health accounts. I especially loved working with sales and marketing groups and traveling the country.

Conducting a fitness training program at Peat Marwick in 1989.

I owe tremendous gratitude to an organization founded in the mid-1980s that helped women build their businesses — American Women's Economic Development (AWED), a non-profit corporation. Times were changing and women were running their own businesses and needed training to make them successful. I joined a "manage your own business" training program which officially lasted for a year and a half. However, seven of us continued to meet for many years. We were small businesses in different fields. We met about every six weeks for 10 years and then less frequently. We reviewed our businesses, marketing, finances, and personnel issues. We brought our problems to one another, shared professional development trainings, and celebrated successes. In fact, we had established our own personal advisory board, and I have always recommended to any woman that she get her own personal advisory board to call on. Whether it's to look at her resume or to help solve a business problem or decision to be made, a personal advisory board of peers can make all the difference.

One story in particular illustrates how sexism in the workplace was changing. In 1991 when working a large sales conference, a trainer started his address to more than 150 sales and marketing managers with a dirty joke. The women managers, about 15% of the room, walked out and complained to the national field director, a male. He then walked into the room, strode up onto the stage and summarily fired the well-paid trainer. That made a lasting impression on me. It showed that the male leadership would not tolerate this behavior (women managers were vital to the company's success) and women should collectively take a position against it. That was a lesson for the women and for everybody. Times were changing.

I was grateful for my Dad, who always coached me, because I can't recall ever having any women come on the campus and talk to us about women in business or women in the government. I don't know if a career office even existed. Today, the Career Services Office at Penn offers extraordinary resources and training for Penn students and alums.

Motherhood: The Other Side of a Woman's Life
I balanced my work and family with part-time work, working on my own, and with the help of my parents. Somehow I made it through, working, raising my boys and caring for a mother with cancer. In the late 1980s, when I worked with corporations and women had babies, they got only six weeks maternity leave and treated kids like a secret. They didn't feel comfortable talking about their children. Women in my stress management courses complained that guys had no problems leaving the office early to coach their kids' sports. The women said, "What's wrong with this picture? I have to keep my child under wraps while they're talking about their kids all the time and it was okay for them to take off." That's how insecure women were forced to be about having a family and working in the late 1980s.

The Trustees Council of Penn Women (TCPW)
The Trustees' Council of Penn Women was formed 30 years ago by then chairman of the Board of Trustees, Al Shoemaker. He looked at the development statistics and said, "We have most of our money coming from men graduates; women are not giving like alumnae of single-sex women's' colleges. We're not doing enough for women."

Judy Roth Berkowitz invited me to join the Council and I've been honored to be a member for thirty years. I've been at the university twice a year for Trustees Council meetings. I worked on promoting the advancement of women and witnessed how Penn has progressed.

The Trustees Council meets at Penn twice a year and has an assigned staff person from alumni relations. The Trustees Council was set up to succeed: you had to be invited to join, donate a certain amount of money, and work on a committee. We award grants and offer all kinds of support to make an impact. Altogether, the women who have been on the Trustees Council over the years have donated over $350 million.

We work closely with the provost's office, getting reports, asking for reports and pushing for the advancement of women faculty. We have spotlighted improving women's safety and health — like preventing food disorders — and presented Career Nights and other programs.

We pushed the University and supported the women faculty to have onsite childcare and to change some of the requirements for gaining tenure. (A professor is supposed to be doing significant publishing exactly at the time when a woman is fertile and wants to start a family. Time was a hurdle.)

The Trustees Council also has become the pipeline for leadership for women at the University. Once you become a member of the Trustees Council, you could move onto one of the Boards of Overseers. Each board requires a certain level of donation. You don't just get on it, especially one like Wharton, which carries the highest donation level.

A few years ago, one of the worst decisions I believe the Trustees Council of Penn Women executive committee made was to follow the university's new ruling that a member on the Board of Trustees must become emerita at age 70. TCPW members now also automatically became emerita at 70. The committee wanted to make slots available for new members, but they have lost the institutional memories and vitality of the founding and older members. We can attend, even be on a committee, but no longer have to pay dues. There was never a vote on this critical issue by the entire council, and it came as a shock to me. We were founded to fight gender discrimination and now practice age discrimination. Some women don't care, but I like the involvement and still contribute my knowledge, ideas and network. Although I pushed hard against this policy, it has remained.

Women practicing age discrimination is poor policy. I'll continue to work on TCPW and be co-president of my class, but I feel Penn is sending out the message, "We want your money but when you turn 70, we don't want you anymore." It's disappointing and not right in my opinion.

Life's Lessons As I Moved On — Norway Became My Reality

By 1992 I was transitioning to work in Professional Development and as a Personal Marketing and Career Coach. At the same time, Norway entered my life.

Since my Outward Bound courses, I have hiked mountains all over the U.S., Europe and Africa, including climbing Mr. Kilimanjaro in 1984. In 1992, I went on two hiking trips in Norway, fell in love with the country and a Norwegian, and have gone back often to what has become my

"second home." I helped a mountaineer develop his marketing materials for the United States and was invited to give a talk on hiking and cross country skiing at the Sons of Norway fraternal lodge in Manhattan in 1996. A year later

Me (fourth from left) with fellow Sons of Norway lodge members in New York.

I became president of the lodge and continued as a leader for twenty years, building membership, presenting programs and working with the Consuls General. (I'm not a son, not a Norwegian, but all of my Norwegian involvement just felt right in my gut.)

I became a writer and columnist for the New York-based *Norway Times*, a Norwegian/American newspaper, which I did for ten years. I decided to learn Norwegian and attended the International Summer School (ISS) of the University of Oslo from 1997 to 1999.

The school has 550 students from 98 countries, many of them interesting adults in their 20s to 40s. I proposed teaching a professional development seminar and convinced the ISS that this was much needed by the graduate level students. ISS accepted and I have been teaching this experiential, non-academic, extracurricular seminar with great joy since 2000. I also created a marketing plan for ISS in America to fundraise for scholarships. One-fifth of ISS is composed of Americans. It's been deeply satisfying, and I'm still teaching every summer.

Full Circle

I said initially that I have a love of learning about foreign cultures, and here I am teaching the world's cultures. I've taught people from all over the globe—India, China, Brazil, Kurdistan, Afghanistan, Nepal, Azerbaijan, Tanzania, and Uganda.

Me (front center) with my Norwegian language students in 2008.

My students work in media, healthcare, energy, education and diplomatic posts, etc. Teaching in Norway has become my passion. I love to work with people, to teach and see students grow, help them make career decisions and solve problems. My career has been like a rolling stone gathering no moss. It has taken me in different directions, but teaching and organizing new initiatives reflecting my values remains at my core. I do what feels right in my gut.

In addition to ISS, since 2000 I have been a project manager of a Girl Scout program in East Harlem for underserved families, sponsored by my Unitarian Church. The four troops, 13 Leaders and 50 scouts use my planning, organizing and teaching skills to develop the girls' life-long values and commitment. My life has all come together!

Reflections

These reflections are lessons I learned and they helped me live a life I love.

- Many of the women in our class had an intertwining with their husbands and a safe platform to launch businesses, careers, and raise families. As Sheryl Sandberg said in her book, *Lean In*, "One of the most important decisions that woman will make is the man she marries." My marriage, though relatively short, reflected this and helped shape my adult life.

• Penn gave me the foundation, the education and special experiences with international students. It offered me a network of friends and a relationship with the University which continues today. Among my friends from the class of 1964 is Connie McNeely Horner, my suitemate at Hill House, who, when head of the federal Bureau of Personal Management, used my company Fitness by Fisher as part of a national conference. Classmates Diana Abazzia Holdridge, Susan Jimison Viteck and I volunteered together at the 2012 and 2016 Democratic National Conventions. My life has been enriched, forming friendships while working together on alumni initiatives (I'm co-president of the Class of 1964 and co-chaired our 50th Reunion) and TCPW.

• I did experience some gender inequality. I swam in Weightman Hall pool, in the "women's gym," It definitely was second rate compared to the men's. The Penguinnettes — my synchronized swim team — was allowed to use the beautiful Olympic-size men's pool only for our big show. I remember thinking, "How come the guys got all this good stuff?"

• We lived at Penn *in loco parentis*, with its behavioral rules, regulations and punishments. These are totally unacceptable in 2018, but we never thought to challenge them. Since the late 1960s, though, I've been a tiger.

• Another opportunity that really made a change in my life was the "Experiment in International Living" in Mexico in 1963. Richard encouraged me to do this, as he had been on the Experiment to France. France was too costly for me, but Mexico cost the least at $400. I usually worked in the summers to help pay for school, but I just knew this program had the potential to change my life, so I took a loan (this later established my credit) and went to Mexico. I even rented Richard my motor scooter for $50 for the summer while he worked for the Experiment in NYC. Every dollar counted!

• Another interesting experience was when I asked my father-in-law if he would give me $10,000 to run for a political office. It was for the experience and not a winnable seat. He declined. His company also never allowed any of the women of the family to work in the family business. Men only.

• Racial and religious divisiveness are more open throughout the country, particularly in the north, through social media in 2018 than the 1960s. Make a stand for civil rights, womens' rights, and civility.

• Like others, I've had many stressful and anxiety-provoking experiences. For me the best help was from a gifted psychoanalyst who guided me through tumultuous waters. I've worked with some duds too, but overall the good experiences with psychotherapy have helped my children and me immeasurably. I encourage you to get help if you need it, and don't stop looking until you find the right person!

• Remember to thank your parents and everyone else who helps you along the way to achieve your dream, or watch your sick children while you must work.

• I think to be a success as a person, you need competence, good communication skills, curiosity, respect for others, honesty, trustworthiness, and an ability to develop opportunities and find the silver-lining. You also need to be the best child, parent, sibling and friend possible. (Sounds like the Girl Scout Law and Promise!) Whatever experiences you have add to your life experience; they give you breadth and make you a more interesting and, hopefully, wiser human being.

LESLIE GALLERY-DILWORTH

A ZIGZAG PATH TO FAR-REACHING
ACCOMPLISHMENTS IN ARCHITECTURE

No matter who you are or what you're doing, if you see a problem, you can turn it into an opportunity to initiate something which makes permanent change happen. When you think, "Someone should do something about this," well, that somebody can and should be you.

The concept that, as a female, there were limitations on what I could do or become was <u>never</u> part of my upbringing or even my vocabulary. I wanted to be an architect from the time I was 10, when I first saw Frank Lloyd Wright's Mile High Building proposal in the newspaper.

Leslie Gallery-Dilworth

My Early Years
My father played a major role in my becoming an architect and in thinking beyond sexual stereotypes. He was in the home building business. Starting when I was six years old, he would take me with him to job sites and ask the workmen to explain to me what they were doing. At age 8, I told him I wanted to be a stewardess, and his response was, "You do not want to be a stewardess, you want to be the pilot." My father actually gave me an ivory 6-inch slide rule as my Sweet 16 birthday present. (I still have it, although I have never mastered it.) Growing up in Pottsville, Pa., a very small town in rural central Pennsylvania, and later in Reading, Pa., there was only one high school. When I wanted to take a drafting class or a shop class, which were for boys only, the teachers would not let me, because they said I would be distracting to the boys. I pestered the teachers and, finally, they allowed me to take the class privately, during study hall.

Architecture School – Round One
From high school I was accepted into the architecture programs at Case Western Reserve University in Cleveland, Ohio, and Syracuse University in New York. I chose Case Western. At the time, 1960, schools of architecture proudly advertised that girl students were limited to only 10% of the class. Because the classes were very small, the average was 2.5 women per school. Classes as an architecture major began at 8 a.m. and

went without a break until 6 p.m. every day. At the end of my freshman year, I received a D in Introduction to Architectural Design. It wasn't for lack of trying. I had worked very hard and was very disappointed. When my dad saw my grades, he was very concerned and wanted to know why I had received such a poor grade. He called the professor and arranged for us to fly out to meet with my teacher. I was, of course, horrified at the prospect.

My father explained to my professor he wasn't questioning the grade; he just wanted to understand how my work related to the other students. The professor showed us some students' work which received an A; then my Dad asked him to show us some C projects, and to explain how his daughter's projects compared. The professor became flustered and admitted there really was no difference; however, the professor continued, "Someone has to decide who's going to make it and who's not, and I'm going to tell you she's never going to make it as an architect."

My father replied, "What gives you the right to say to a 17-year-old what she will or won't accomplish in her life?" Furthermore, he said, "If Leslie wants to become an architect, she will, and no one is going to stand in her way, certainly not you." Then he turned to me and said, "Come on, Leslie, we're leaving. There's no point in our talking to him any further."

In 1990, I was elected to the College as Fellows of the American Institute of Architects, one of the few women to achieve that recognition. The professor never was elected to the AIA College of Fellows.

My Transfer to Penn and a New Course Major

In my sophomore year, I switched my major to art history and medieval studies and received mostly As. Then I applied to transfer to Penn for my junior year. Only seven transfer students were being accepted. The Dean of Women interviewed me. Based on my transcript, I had little chance of being accepted. At one point, I noticed a large drawing of the Santa Sophia basilica in Istanbul behind the Dean's desk. I asked, "Why do you have a drawing of Hagia Sophia?" She replied, "Oh, I'm from Turkey. How do you know about that?" I answered, "It's my favorite building." After that we had a great conversation about Byzantine architecture, Middle Eastern archeology, and the collection at the University Museum. As we said goodbye, she accepted me on the spot.

The Serendipity Continues

Many years later, in 1988, a similar event took place when I was consulting on an architecture project in London. I was involved in a program to bring together local architects and Prince Charles, and establish a Foundation for Architecture as I had done in Philadelphia.

The Prince had been very critical of the city's new architecture, and established his own school of architecture. I was in his assistant's office, waiting for a meeting, when I saw behind her desk a very high contrast photograph of the gardens of Villa Lante in central Italy. I commented to her about the image, asking her if it was the Villa Lante. She said, "Yes, how could you tell?" I said, "Oh, I used to teach the history and theory of landscape architecture at the University of Texas, and this is my absolute favorite renaissance garden and villa." "Really?" she responded. "Have you been there?" "No, I haven't been there, but I'd really like to go."

"Well," she said. "It just so happens we're having our summer program there this year, and we need a professor of landscape architecture. Would you be interested?" I replied immediately, "Of course I'd be interested!" I spent several weeks on the faculty of Prince Charles' international program. On the last night, Prince Charles hosted a very small dinner in the villa for the students and faculty, about 25. I was seated next to him.

My Job Interviews in New York City and My First Job After College—1964

During my senior year at Penn, I applied to many different graduate programs, in architecture, landscape architecture, history of art, and medieval studies. But in each application I managed to omit one thing or another; hence, no action could be taken. John McCoubrey, the respected professor of modern art, was my advisor. He said, "If only you could put both your feet in the same pan of water at the same time, you could be very successful!" He was very good natured about writing so many letters of recommendation. David Robb, professor of medieval art, also was very encouraging.

Since I was so undecided and uncommitted, immediately after graduation I did what was expected of bright liberal arts majors: I went to a one-month secretarial school. I flunked shorthand, and I barely got by in typing. Then I went to New York City over the summer, as many young women did. My interviews were eye opening and, in retrospect, quite comical. One interviewer asked me if I had been a homecoming queen or in a sorority. I said no and asked, "Why are you asking me these questions?" She said, "Because we find that girls who have been homecoming queens or active in a sorority make better sales representatives for us." I said, "I know a lot about architecture and building." She said, "We don't care about that." The job was for a sales rep for architectural products.

Every place I went, my typing wasn't fast enough, so they wouldn't even let me in the door. Finally I did get in the door at a major advertising agency. I was sitting in the waiting room and I noticed the boys were being called to go to the left door, and the girls were going to the right door.

I went to the receptionist and I said, "Why are the girls going to the right door and the boys are going to the left door?" She said, "That's our executive training program to the left." I asked, "What's to the right?" She said, "That's our secretarial program." I said, "Well I don't want to be a secretary. I want to go in the executive training program." "Oh no, no," she said, "Girls are not allowed."

Then I had another interview arranged by a friend with the director of the Guggenheim Museum. At the end of the interview, he said, "We'd love to hire you." I asked, "What is the salary?" He told me. I responded, "I can't live on $50.00 a week." He said, "Oh, you're not supposed to, my dear. It's expected your parents will continue to support you. That's how all of our girls are hired at the Guggenheim." I said, "Unfortunately, my parents are not expecting that, so I guess this isn't going to work."

Finally, I was at Hearst Publications for an interview, and my typing test was one word too low for them to consider me. The personnel department interviewer said, "We have a woman upstairs who is the Director of Marketing and Research. She doesn't like anybody we've ever sent her, so I have nothing to lose by sending you to meet her."

I met the Director in her office. She was the highest ranking woman in advertising and marketing at that time — not just at Hearst, but in all of New York. She said to me, "I have only one question for you: If I were out to lunch, it was 3:00 in the afternoon, and I wasn't back yet, and Mr. Hearst called, what would you say?" "I would say you had just stepped out of the office for a minute, and you'd be right back. I would have you call as soon as you walked back in." She said, "You're hired." I asked, "Why?" She said, "Because the last person who worked here when Mr. Hearst called and it was 3:00, she said, "Oh, Ms. Harris is not back from lunch yet."

Part of my job was reading all the magazines that Hearst published. The other part was a lot of statistical typing. I had to produce six copies of columns of numbers, using carbon paper. I am dyslexic, so I wasted a lot of paper. Each day I came to work with a bigger pocketbook and finally a shopping bag so I could take home the wasted paper, rather than have anyone see it in the trash baskets. At the end of the summer, I came to the conclusion this job was not for me and decided to go back to graduate school in landscape architecture. The Director said to me, "Leslie, you are the best secretary I have ever had, provided you can have your own typist."

My Return to Penn and Landscape Architecture School

Just before classes were to begin at Penn, I called Ian McHarg, the chair of the Department of Landscape Architecture. He admitted me to the graduate school for landscape architecture. The first year was very, very hard, both physically and emotionally. I was not prepared; I lacked the basic skills. The other students, many of whom were from India and England, already had degrees in architecture. I think I stuck it out because my father used to tell me stories about when he was a test pilot, how the instructors tried to wash everyone out, and how he just kept hanging in no matter how hard it was.

One night, in the first month of graduate school when we were doing this really complex project as a team, my team (all boys except for me) had come up with horrible designs. In the middle of the night I looked at what they had put out and I thought, "This is awful. I can do a lot better than this. Why am I just following them?"

All during the night I just worked really hard and redesigned the whole project, which was called Schuylkill South, a big area in Philadelphia. I made all the models even though I had never used a saw before. When my teammates came in the next day, they were just flabbergasted, as were the teachers. Because of my work and redesign, we received an A on the project. I think I learned a lot from that experience, as did the boys on my team. I didn't have to take a backseat to anyone, and they had new respect for me.

After two semesters in landscape architecture, I still wasn't doing really well. I was demoralized, and exhausted. I did not give up, but I did need a change. Looking through magazines in the fine arts library, I noticed architects and landscape architects were doing interesting work in Israel, and some of the professionals had ties to Penn. I went to work for a firm in Haifa, Israel, for the summer. In Israel there were many women in architecture and landscape architecture. The environment and the people were absolutely invigorating. I returned to school refreshed and ready to confront the challenges with a new attitude and self-confidence.

Then I happened to see the only woman Penn professor in architecture, Stanislava Nowicki, who was a major force in just about every architecture student's life. She asked me where I had been, and why she hadn't seen me in the architecture studio. I told her I was in the landscape architecture program. She said, "That's really a shame because you have a real talent and a real sense of what architecture is, and you should switch into architecture." And that's what I did. In retrospect, I realize I was reluctant to confront the architecture program because I was afraid of failing. But once I was in the program, I thrived. While it was very hard, I was invigorated by the challenge.

Although it was a very tumultuous time on the international and national scene, I don't recall there being any big disruptions on the Penn campus; but we all shared a real sense of service to the community, and of hope and optimism. For me, it was of being able to improve society through architecture, design, and planning. I was passionate and committed to the impact architecture could have on all our lives, and in all places.

After graduation from architecture school in 1968, I went to San Francisco to visit some friends and look for a job. I had eight offers when people were not getting even one, because I was from Penn, then the top-ranked architecture school in the country. I took a job in San Francisco with a respected and well-known firm, Moore Turnbull Lyndon and Whitaker. Soon I learned I was being paid five cents an hour less than a guy who was hired at the same time. So I did bring that little problem to the head of the firm.

I was the only woman in my Master's Studio with Louis Kahn (he's at lower left).

Nevertheless, they gave me considerable responsibility: to design a big house and to do the interior of a house at the new development, The Sea Ranch, in California.

I came back from California and went back to graduate school — to Louis Kahn's Master's Studio. During that same time, 1970, I did a lot of work with a group called the Young Great Society (YGS), a community group located in a residential neighborhood north of the Penn campus. At the time, the community was plagued by dangerous rival gangs. The YGS had a Planning and Design Center, as well as different kinds of community projects. The YGS planning center was run by professional designers who were recent graduates from Penn. They put me in charge of specifying new plantings for the vacant lots.

The children in the neighborhood noticed me surveying the vacant lots, and started to follow me around. They were interested in what I was doing. I created a program for the neighborhood kids. Very quickly, we were developing all kinds of activities, such as collecting plant samples and learning math by figuring out the number of plants for that particular species in that section of the vacant lot. Then we involved the teenage boys. In one of the three big gangs I worked with, every gang member had been in prison for manslaughter. My strategy was to give them each a leadership role so they would gain a feeling of accomplishment and satisfaction by contributing something of value to others. I trained them all to be teachers to the younger local kids. They each would receive a certificate. Then they could become the teachers in the neighborhood schools to give instruction about the plants and animals that were indigenous to their neighborhood.

A *Philadelphia Bulletin* reporter was interested in the project and asked one 14-year-old, "What interests you about the weeds?" This boy answered, "Well, I guess the weeds are kind of like us. They manage to survive when nothing else can." What a moment!

I already had one master's degree; at the time it was called a Bachelor of Architecture because it was a first professional degree, just like a law degree. When I finished with graduate school, I had earned graduate degrees in architecture, a Masters in Louis Kahn's studio, and had completed all course work in the master's program in landscape architecture. Of the 400-plus students who completed the Master's Studio with Lou Kahn, only 14 were women.

My City Gardens Business
One day, while walking through the Old City section of Philadelphia, I noticed that beautiful old buildings were gradually being torn down. I felt I had to do something to help save Philadelphia's old buildings and show how they could be transformed to mixed uses.

 I convinced my then boyfriend to take all his money — $30,000 — and invest in renovating one of the old warehouses. No bank would give us a loan. They said, "Who would ever want to live or work in a warehouse or a loft?" We decided to take over the building ourselves, and because we needed immediate income from the space, with $2,500 we opened a garden center on the first floor. It was June, and we had to be in business by late August in order to capture the fall planting market.

I worked out a scheme with a New Jersey nursery to supply plants and do all the planting, and that's how I opened City Gardens. It was the first retail store in that part of the city and the very first garden center that catered specifically to city gardens; it became quite successful. I put my design studio right there so people could look over the rail and see me.

My City Gardens

This resulted in garden design jobs and renovations. I learned a lot about hiring and firing and running a business. I thought of City Gardens as an indoor urban park. We also held classes for high school students and workshops with the horticultural society.

Moving On – Marriage and Teaching

My mother said, "Well now that you have finished all of this architecture stuff, don't you think now it's time to get married?"

I never thought of myself as being married or having children. It was not a priority or a goal. I aspired to be an architect, designing interesting buildings and projects. But I did get married when I was 30.

In 1973 we moved to Austin, Texas, because my husband was offered a job as the Associate Dean of the Architecture and Planning Department and as the Chairman of the Planning Department at the University of Texas. They offered me a job teaching. At my first meeting with the provost, I said, "I want to teach full time." He said, "You can't teach full time here because of the nepotism rule. Your husband is the Associate Dean, and wives are allowed to teach only part time if they are in the same department." After the first semester, I got a special dispensation from the Board of Regents to allow me to teach full time.

In graduate school at Penn, there was never one sign of discrimination. Actually, the girls were always the best in the class because it was so hard for women to get in. There were only three girls in each class, yet there was no discussion in the classroom or in seminars about women in the workplace, nor about entrepreneurship. There were no successful women architects at the time who could be invited to speak to Penn classes.

I really didn't understand or feel discrimination until after Penn. At the University of Texas, I started an organization, called The Women's Faculty Caucus, to fight sex discrimination. There were no maternity leave policies. A married women was not allowed to have a charge account in her own name, or own a car in her own name even if she paid for it. I became active in the leadership of the Women's Equity Action League (WEAL), and changing these policies was an important and successful goal.

In the early 1970s, when women's lib was really taking off and *Ms. Magazine* first came out, I had read that the number of women in architecture was so small they couldn't even show it as an integer percentage even though there were percentages assigned to women engineers, lawyers and doctors. At faculty meetings, documents would refer to "he" in everything that was handed out. I would raise my hand and say, "Excuse me, I just want to remind you 'architect' is not the name of the sex, it is a profession."

Discrimination Carries Forward–A Personal Note
We taught at the University of Texas for four years, and then I had my first child. When a woman has children, the landscape really changes. Because of the pressures of an architecture firm, it was (and still is) very difficult and challenging to run a professional practice and be a caring responsible mother. This should be a parents' issue, not a mother's issue. Teaching was a good environment for being a good mother. When I moved back to Philadelphia in 1978 and wanted to resume a career as an architect, there was little, if any, daycare. And of course, all the men in the architecture firms had wives (which was what I needed). When my second son was about 6 months old, I was desperate to get back into the profession; I loved my children, but I also loved architecture. I heard the position of Director of the Philadelphia chapter of the American Institute of Architects (AIA) was open. AIA had never hired a woman, and I didn't have any confidence they'd hire me. But my husband strongly urged me to go after this job. I consulted with the planner and architect Denise Scott Brown, who was married to Robert Venturi. She coached me through the interview process, especially what to say when the board of architects asked me about my children.

She advised me to say, "You're all married and you all have children, and you all managed to be successful in your work. I will too." That's exactly what I said. But they persisted, noting that there is travel involved and asking who would take care of the kids. I said, "Legally,

you're not allowed to ask that, but I'm happy to answer." If I hadn't answered it, they would never have hired me. I did get the job.

The AIA Interview Committee pointed out that my husband had an important job in Philadelphia as Director of Housing and Community Development and Planning. Their question was, what I would I do if he had an opinion different from the AIA? I responded that I often have a different professional opinion from my husband. I don't think they ever would have asked that of a man.

Good childcare is a huge challenge. Just to be safe, we always had two au pairs at the house all the time; one to live in and one to come every day.

The AIA Foundation for Architecture
Shaping my work environment around my family responsibilities and priorities is what has been consistent throughout my career. My priority was integrating my family and my work. Therefore, I had to create and design my work environment and my jobs.

One of my most important early accomplishments at AIA was to initiate the chapter's Foundation for Architecture. I really enjoy putting together a board, working with a board, and putting together a team.

In Philadelphia I was on several boards. Two of the boards I enjoyed most were the Friends of the Philadelphia Museum of Art and the Fairmount Park Historic Houses. I really love to build organizations and to make ideas happen, like the city's sign program. One day, driving back from the Philadelphia airport, I got lost because the sign directions were so confusing. I was so angry and concerned that I made it a priority to have designed and installed a whole new directional and attraction signage system. The project included working on all the funding, maintenance and legislation, as well as design. That program is still in place. Later I initiated similar programs in Newark, N.J., in Wilmington, Del., and in Miami Beach, Fla.

You can make change happen and you can make an important contribution to your community.

My Life After the Foundation for Architecture

I had founded the Foundation for Architecture in Philadelphia, an innovative influential civic organization with major funding from Dr. Otto Haas, CEO of Rohm and Haas, and other civic leaders. After five years — after leading the

An example of the signage program I initiated. That's me on the right.

organization from a budget of $2,500 to one of $2.5 million, from a staff of 0.5 to 18, and from zero members to 1200 — I wanted to move on. I met with Dr. Haas, who asked me, "What do you want to do next? Just write it down on one page and attach a budget." Dr. Haas read over the proposal and said, "I'll fund this." I was given a $300,000 grant from the Otto Haas Foundation to travel worldwide and think about architecture and urban planning. From that work, I was selected as a USA fellow, the mid-career fellowship from the National Endowment for the Arts.

A few years later, I was contacted by leaders of the Society for Environmental Graphic Design, a respected international membership organization of leading designers. The organization had fallen on hard times. This was an opportunity to rebuild a once respected organization. Among our accomplishments, in addition to building a stable financial base, was the production of 25 issues of an elegant magazine, *segdDesign*.

I thought I'd be there one year just to turn it around, but I stayed there for 12 years until I retired. My strongest ability is to put together a good team. So whenever we had an idea, we were able to implement it.

Then I began writing books and speaking. My first book was Luck Is Not a Plan for Your Future, Design Your Tomorrow Today. I am working on my second book, 70 $-E-N-$-E, 7 Decades of Wit and Wisdom for Women.

Turning Problems Into Opportunities

The year 1964 was a real turning point for women. It was still part of the old school while we were stepping into the new school.

One of the most the most important decisions and choices a woman can make, if you want to have a successful career, is whom you marry. Your partner has to really want you to have a successful career as much as you do. He has to agree to split the home care responsibilities with you, at least in half.

My education gave me the courage and the confidence to keep moving on. I think the most important thing is the graduate school you attend. Not only is that network very influential, but the quality of the graduate school can give you immediate credibility to get your foot in the door. Having degrees from Penn was very helpful.

My early career goal of designing skyscrapers, and designing parks and cities, was not directly met; however, in this zig zag path, I know that I have influenced communities, design, women and families, and of that I am happy.

CLAIRE GORDON

AN OUTSTANDING CORPORATE CAREER BRINGS ENTREPRENEURIAL OPPORTUNITIES

As we are all well aware, the early Sixties was a time of major change in America. Civil rights were being challenged....and protested...and legislated. And along with civil change came new roles for women both in the home and in the workplace.

So at Penn in the Sixties, the class of '64 was on the cusp of this revolution. We can now reflect on the impact this time in our lives had on the various paths we took and who we are today.

Claire Israel Gordon

My Early Years

I grew up in Philadelphia, Pa., and since I qualified for a competitive, city-wide magnet school — the Philadelphia High School for Girls — my parents insisted I attend. It took an hour by public transportation to get to school and I certainly resisted — to no avail. There were 130 girls in our class — black and white, from different backgrounds, varying economic levels and all religions. We were totally unaware of these differences. We were all smart and competitive but worked as a team and pulled each other up. One classmate became the first female head of the Black Panthers (her boyfriend was Bobby Seale). Another is a world renowned physician and research professor. The bar was set high — very high.

The guidance counselor dissuaded all of us from going to local colleges as she wanted the "Girls' High" name to get representation at prestigious universities around the country. However because our class graduated in January, I applied to Penn as it was one of the few universities to have mid-year admission.

My parents told me to choose whatever major I wanted. They insisted, however, that I have a profession when I graduated and wanted me to obtain a teaching certificate, which I did. My dad had graduated from college but, due to the "Great Depression," my mom did not, and she always regretted she couldn't continue her studies. In retirement, my parents audited courses at local universities and often bumped into their grandchildren on Penn's campus. These are very special memories for my parents and my children as well.

70

Education at Penn

I was a Sociology major and Math minor. By combining these two studies, I worked for a brilliant and wonderful demography professor, Dr. Philip Sagi. In those days, we were using punched cards and electronic sorters for research. This method was cumbersome, time consuming and inefficient. Dr. Sagi urged me to go to the Moore School of Engineering at Penn where the ENIAC computer was located and on display. A newer computer also was there and available to the professors for research.

At Moore, I was handed three program instruction books — COBOL (for business applications), FORTRAN (for scientific applications) and RPG (a proprietary IBM program language for business applications). There were no classes in programming and everyone learned by reading — and trial and error. In the movie, *Hidden Figures,* set in 1961, NASA distributed these identical FORTRAN instruction books to their mathematicians to expedite their sending John Glenn into space.

This was an amazing time to do research as we transitioned from rudimentary computational systems to a new world with the invention of electronic computers. By today's standards, these main frames were slow and mammoth, but we were on the cusp of a technical revolution, for sure.

Early Career

In the spring of 1964, my fellow classmate Ron Gordon (now my husband of 51 years) told me IBM was coming to the Wharton School to recruit. I signed up for an interview simply by putting my name on a time sheet hanging on a wall in Dietrich Hall. When I was offered a job as an IBM Systems Engineer in Philadelphia, I was told

Me with Ron.

(and, yes, these were the exact words), "If a woman can understand a computer, no man would be intimidated." My pay was 10% less than the men's, but in those days I wasn't offended. I just felt I had to work a little harder to rise above! I loved working for IBM, and I quickly caught up to the men's salaries.

Memphis – 1966

Ron and I married in 1965 during the Vietnam war. Ron joined a Naval Air Reserve unit and was flown to Memphis on an unpressurized military plane for boot camp. Without any parental guidance or help, I had to move to Memphis, find a place for us to live and get a job. And in those days we rarely called home, as phone calls were expensive.

IBM had no office in Memphis but set up interviews for me with companies that had IBM computers, and I took a job with Union Planters Bank. Selling the computer services of the bank to their large commercial customers was a major learning experience. Working and living in Memphis in the Sixties certainly impacted who I am today — being independent, selling rather than being a "techy," witnessing the KKK, enjoying the Southern culture and experiencing the military mentality!

My Career Continues

After Memphis, we moved to Cincinnati. My husband had accepted a job in marketing with Procter & Gamble, and IBM transferred me to their

branch there. When our first child was born, I left IBM to work part-time as a systems analyst in the healthcare industry: first with the Cincinnati Hospital Council which was a planning and oversight agency, and then with an HEW tri-state (Ohio, Kentucky and Indiana) planning and review board. The health care industry in the 70s was dealing with many of the same issues as today — cost containment, bioethical questions, childhood immunizations, computerized record keeping, privacy, etc. Systems analysis in the health care industry was intellectually challenging, and the resulting guidelines are often the benchmark today.

After almost 17 years in Cincinnati, we moved to Connecticut when my husband changed companies. Although I was planning on staying in the health field, I was offered an exciting opportunity to design a computer system for a magazine reprint company that was being launched.

After setting up the system, I started calling on magazines in New York City. I loved it and headed up sales for many years. I enjoyed dealing with the printing plant and meeting with the magazine publishers. It

72

was an exciting career change that gave me flexibility while raising our children. However, as copyright customs changed and technologies improved, companies started producing their own reprints and the industry slowed, then stopped.

An Entrepreneurial Turn
Through a confluence of circumstances, I got the exclusive right to sell a unique item — over-the-counter pince-nez reading glasses. As an entrepreneur, I quickly had to learn all elements of establishing a business — trademarks, packaging, accounting, QVC fulfillment, catalog marketing, website design, shipping, etc. I did it all and enjoyed every aspect of this intense, entrepreneurial experience for many years.

What To Do Next?
Starting in my twenties, I had always volunteered for not-for-profit organizations and eventually served on various boards, something my children emulate.

At Penn, I continue to be an emeritus member of the Trustees Council of Penn Women and have served on the Board of the Penn Club of New York since its founding. I have been Program Chairperson at both of these Penn affiliations and have been an active member of other committees as well.

Additionally, over the years, I've been on boards relating to the arts, religious organizations, educational institutions and community services. As of this writing, I am about to begin serving on the board of a Connecticut agency that provides continuity of care for the elderly who want to "age in place" and remain in their homes. This is an area of interest to me, as I've had extensive experience in managing my parents' care. As the Class of '64 ages, elder care issues and legislation seem especially relevant.

Continuing Education
Although I wanted to get an MBA, I was always on overload with work and family responsibilities. There were courses I felt would expand my knowledge and confidence, but not necessarily further my career. Now, as a senior citizen, I've been taking "lifelong learning" courses — Mindfulness, Beer making, Painting, Bridge — to name a few.

At a local university, I recently took a thought provoking course in Bioethics taught by the chair of the Philosophy department. Fortunately, I have had the opportunity to hear many lectures by Dr. Arthur Caplan, former chairman of the prestigious Bioethics department at Penn. These interdisciplinary studies at Penn, involving law, medicine and philosophy, might be my major if I were matriculating at Penn today.

The Penn Experience — Impact on the Future

The road not taken…who knows? Certainly, Penn remains the keystone of my life even 50+ years after graduation. My husband and I met at Penn. My career started as an undergraduate at Penn. Both our children decided Penn was their first choice of a university ('91 and '95), without any pressure from us. And many of our friends today are those we met more than a half a century ago.

Celebrating with Ron at our 50th reunion

Advice to Penn Students

Perhaps these words of wisdom from my dad on his 100th birthday will say it all…

Phil's Top 10 Tips for Living to 100

10. Eat a BIG breakfast
9. Don't dwell on "Yesterday's News"
8. Keep your body moving
7. Learn something new every day
6. Make the world a better place
5. Work hard…and enjoy play
4. Surround yourself with beauty
3. Roll with the punches
2. Great partner….family & friends & support
1. Mazel (Luck)

EDA L. HOCHGELERENT, M.D.

A TALENTED NEPHROLOGIST FINDS PERSONAL AND PROFESSIONAL FULFILLMENT

I suppose we all have known the "pioneering" spirit as we have followed our career paths. I have been very fortunate to have known great fulfillment personally and professionally.

Eda L. Hochgelerent, M.D.

Overview
I became a physician. It was my dream for so many years, and I saw no reason why it could not be possible. There were three women in my class at Penn who became physicians. In the fifty-plus years since we graduated from Penn, many women now are choosing a career in medicine. Women now make up about fifty percent of students in medical schools. There were ten women in my medical school class (10% of my class). All of us were pursuing our ambition and were not aware of the barriers we might encounter along our path.

I have had a fulfilling life as a physician specializing in internal medicine with a subspecialty in nephrology. It has been a privilege for me to have taken care of many patients over many years, to be part of their lives, to know their fears and their pain and, most important, to earn their trust.

My Early Years
I grew up in West Philadelphia and attended public schools, including the Philadelphia High School for Girls which was academically focused. Philadelphia offered so many wonderful opportunities with its many museums and cultural institutions. I was fortunate to experience much of the diversity in the city. To explore and know a city and watch it change was fascinating for me, and I explored every area of the city. Growing up, my summers were spent at the seashore in New Jersey. Even after living away from Philadelphia for a long period, my husband and I have had a summer home in Stone Harbor, New Jersey, for the past twenty-seven years, where we have been able to enjoy the beach and unwind.

My high school counselors did not influence my choosing Penn for college. West Philadelphia was "my home," and the Penn campus was familiar and comfortable. I was a commuter student and was fortunate to have a car to drive to campus every day. My parents were supportive of my decision to go to Penn and encouraged me in every choice I made. Our long conversations and discussions about every aspect of life from education to politics to cultural events to social change to love and romance provided a foundation for all my life's endeavors.

My mom and dad were both educators. My father was a school counselor. My mother established the in-hospital education program for the Philadelphia Board of Education at the Children's Hospital of Philadelphia (CHOP). She taught hospitalized children there for more than thirty years. My first experience at a hospital was as a candy striper at CHOP when I was thirteen to fourteen years old. I really enjoyed being in the hospital — the sounds, the smells, the activity. During the summer after my high school graduation, I worked in a virology lab at CHOP and learned how it feels to be in a basic research environment.

My parents' dearest friend was our family physician. He was a role model for me. He was so smart about everything! He was kind, gentle, understanding and compassionate. I wanted be just like him. Thus, two great influences in my career path — our dear family friend and my experiences at CHOP.

At Penn
In 1960 when I started at Penn, there were no advisors or counselors for each student, particularly not for commuter students. I chose French as my major because I had excellent language education at the Philadelphia

Bruce (back row) and me (center) at our 50th Penn reunion

High School for Girls, and was able to take advanced placement exams and get college credit at Penn. It therefore was possible to complete my major requirements by the start of my third year. I had to complete basic pre-med courses as well. And, I wanted to take some education classes to get my teaching certificate in Pennsylvania, in case I was not accepted into medical school.

One day, as a sophomore, I received a letter from the Dean of Women, Dr. Jean Brownlee. She noted that my course load was difficult and "seemed disconnected." She suggested I focus on one area — perhaps teaching French at high school or college level as opposed to trying to do all three things. She was kind and solicitous, but I really did not want to change my goal. I wanted to be a doctor. That was my only exposure to career guidance at Penn. I finished all of my classes and requirements at Penn in three and a half years with one summer school session. I graduated with my class in May 1964.

Medical School and Residency
After completing my undergraduate courses in December 1963, I began working full time at Hahnemann Hospital in the pulmonary laboratory as a technician performing arterial blood gas analysis.. I was able to save money for future education and travel. I had applied to two medical schools, Penn and Hahnemann. I was accepted at Hahnemann, but not at Penn. I began classes in September 1964 at Hahnemann, the last step in my schooling toward reaching my professional aim.

There were many stressful times during my four years at Hahnemann University, but I was so involved in learning all the material that was presented that there were few times I was aware of discrimination toward women. There were a few female faculty members. There were some conflicts about skirt lengths and some exclusions of women in the class by male classmates, although it did not seem too significant at that time.

When it came time for internship applications, interviewing was a skill set about which I knew very little. Dress, behavior and networking were all relatively unknown aspects of the process and had never been addressed either in college or medical school. At my interview at Boston City Hospital, one of the prominent physicians who interviewed me told me that there had never been a woman on his service at Boston City Hospital, and he said they did not intend "to start now." So, I meekly said okay and got up from my chair and left his office.

I did my internship from 1968 to 1969 at the University of Texas, San Antonio. It was a demanding experience, working every other night, about one hundred hours per week. I learned so much and felt so empowered when the year ended. A wizened leathered old rancher was admitted to my service one day with fever and cough. He viewed me skeptically. He told me his wife was the only woman who had ever seen him without his clothes on, but said "I guess you will be the second one." Our relationship became a warm and trusting one, after a tentative start!

I did my residency (internal medicine) and fellowship (nephrology) at St. Luke's Hospital of Columbia University, in New York City (1969-1970 and 1971-1973). I did one year in general surgery residency (1970-1971) at Hahnemann. Incidentally, I should point out that when I did the year of surgery, there were no facilities for women, such as locker rooms to change into scrubs. All post-surgery discussions and teaching took place in men's locker rooms after the procedures were completed. It was difficult to overcome these obstacles and the teaching/learning was, therefore, not equitable and I really felt excluded.

Initially, during classes at Penn, one of my professors was involved with the growing peace movement. He encouraged his students to join him on marches. My social and political interests continued when I lived in San Antonio, Texas, during my internship year, with participation in the struggle brewing for civil rights among farm workers. I next moved to New York City for my residency and was involved with anti-Vietnam protests. These years were turbulent and so enlightening for me both professionally and personally. I learned much about civic and civil responsibility.

My Medical Specialty

I decided on nephrology as a subspecialty because it was diagnostically challenging and follow-up with patients was long term, while new procedures such as dialysis and renal transplantation were just being developed. Nephrology offered an exciting combination of approaches to the patient with kidney disease. I had the privilege of being involved in taking care of St. Luke's Hospital's first kidney transplant patient in 1972.

My mentor during my fellowship was the best role model one could ever imagine. He was brilliant, innovative, honest, non-judgmental and kind. After I finished my fellowship, I

Eda (center) with her kidney transplant team.

remained at St. Luke's with a junior faculty appointment at Columbia University. I was consulted to see a patient with kidney disease—a banker, a prominent person in New York City. Apparently even though this patient was very satisfied with my explanations of his disease and plan for diagnosis and treatment, an internist who knew him thought that a young female physician was not the appropriate physician to be directing his care. My mentor wrote a strong letter supporting me and my decisions. Fortunately, things went well and there was no further interference in my patient's care.

My Career Continues

I met my husband, Bruce A. Cassidy, M.D., in 1971. He was a 1970 graduate of Columbia University College of Physicians and Surgeons and came to St. Luke's Hospital as an intern. After his internship, he was drafted and posted to Vietnam. He returned to St. Luke's after the military to finish residency.

We married in July 1974 in Philadelphia on Rittenhouse Square, a short but lovely homecoming in my favorite city. We remained in New York City for another year. My husband then got a fellowship position in pulmonary medicine at Emory University. I was appointed to the Emory Medical School faculty as assistant professor in the division of nephrology and inorganic metabolism. So we moved to Atlanta, Georgia, in July 1975.

Life for me at Emory would prove very interesting. There was a woman senior to me in my division. She is one of the best teachers I have ever known and had an outstanding breadth and understanding of nephrology. I learned that her salary was several thousand dollars less than the salary of her academically equivalent male colleagues. She never brought this inequality to the attention of her superiors—"I never could do it," she said. She had two daughters and did not want to risk threatening her employment. She and I practiced together at Emory Clinic for six wonderful years. We happily had many women medical residents choose our clinical nephrology elective. To this day, I have friends in Atlanta who are practicing medicine and with whom I have warm relationships that began at Emory.

The Dean of the medical school at Emory was a female. To my knowledge, she did not do anything to support women on the faculty, such as supporting equal pay, or supporting equal opportunity for advancement.

Maternity

I became pregnant in 1981, at age 37. My husband and I were very happy, as this was a long wished-for addition to our lives. I had received tenure at Emory after seven years. I asked for a leave of absence in addition to the maternity leave. My colleagues and the head of my division were all happy for me and agreed to cover my patients and teaching responsibilities while I was out.

I went to the Chairman of Medicine and the Dean and asked for a leave of absence without pay for one year. They told me that was not possible. They said "You can take a month's maternity leave, use your vacation time for another month, and then you will have to come back to work." They refused personal leave without pay. Emory's Office of Human Resources was unhelpful.

There was no problem with continuity of care for my patients. I wrote a letter to all members of the medical school faculty and explained my request. In the letter I made it clear that I loved my position and wanted very much to return to it. I asked for a meeting with the president of the university, and he refused to see me. I found myself in a hostile environment when this period should have been a happy time in my life.

I retained a highly skilled employment law and civil rights attorney. He filed charges with the United States Equal Employment Opportunity Commission under Title VII of the 1964 Civil Rights Act. Pregnancy is treated as a disability under the law. Apparently several other faculty members had been granted a leave of absence on the basis of disability. The EEOC found that Emory University did not have an adequate maternity policy in place. Emory University also was in violation of the law in suggesting use of vacation time for maternity leave. This very painful matter was resolved after approximately two years. I received a settlement payment plus my legal fees. Five other women were granted payment for pregnancy-related disability. Emory agreed to develop a new standardized maternity leave policy to be provided to the EEOC within ten days of settlement. I also received an excellent letter of reference from the medical school for future employment. There was to be no further discrimination.

My Fulfilling Career

That was the most hurtful hurdle I have ever faced as a female physician. I have had a wonderful career which has given me great fulfillment. I have followed some patients for more than thirty-five years. The professional and personal relationship is unique, trusting, very intimate and cannot be violated. When I am able to determine what is wrong with a patient and devise a treatment plan, I feel a great sense of accomplishment. All of these medical issues involve life and death. There are no comparable settings in any other profession. Care must be delivered compassionately and with love.

After our daughter's birth, I returned to work initially in an acute/urgent care center where my hours were well defined and scheduled. However, I missed having my own patients. Therefore, I opened my office and resumed private practice, doing internal medicine and nephrology.

Daughter Julia, husband Bruce, and me.

My mother and father moved to Atlanta when our daughter was born. Thus, I never had to worry about child care. Our daughter Julia had the most loving Nana and Baba who enriched her life with art, music, and literature. I was most fortunate and knew that even when things were hectic and perhaps not going well at work, my daughter was safe and all her needs were being met. I am eternally grateful for all that my parents did for my family, especially my daughter. I am acutely aware of the uniqueness of my situation with regard to my daughter's upbringing and realize it is not the norm. Much has been written about work/family responsibility. Each of us must examine our life to determine the best course of action. I hope that society can change to accommodate biologic necessity.

My patient referral lines were largely from other women physicians and many of my female patients and friends. I was affiliated with Piedmont Hospital in Atlanta, and my office was located on the hospital campus in a medical building. I practiced at Piedmont for more than thirty years.

After my husband completed his fellowship at Emory in 1976, he went into private practice of pulmonary medicine, also at Piedmont Hospital. Over the years he became involved in hospital and medical staff administration, ultimately becoming Chairman of the Board of the hospital and the medical center.

Retirement
My husband and I both decided to retire in 2009. Fortunately, I was able to turn my practice over to a young nephrologist who was completing his fellowship at the University of Alabama at Birmingham and wanted to come to practice in Atlanta, where he had grown up. I remained with him for one year in order to effect a smooth transition for my patients.

He has done a great job and is very successful. Coincidentally, his cousin was in my class at the Philadelphia High School for Girls. What a small world!

Since retiring, we have had time to travel. I have worked with the Atlanta Women's Foundation in the Women in Healthcare group. I have worked with the Georgia Transplant Foundation and Kidney Foundation of Georgia over many years as well.

As I reflect on my life over the last half century, I understand many of the choices women face in their careers and in their personal and family life. The hours in medicine are long and the need to keep abreast of current developments is continuous. The emotional and psychological demands of the profession are great. Women in medicine must examine all the priorities which are imposed upon them by their own drives to succeed, their families, and the society in which they live. Women must acquire the means by which to balance personal and professional fulfillment in our society with courage, competence and the will to succeed.

SUSAN HOFFMAN

A CAREER AS AN IBM SYSTEMS ENGINEER

I realize we were pioneers. I'm hoping this book can offer some valuable lessons to women just starting out today.

Susan Miller Hoffman

My Early Education
I went to Northeast High School in Philadelphia, Pa. At the time, it was the best co-ed public high school. Girls High and Central were all female and all male, respectively. We had two honors classes of 25 people each, and I was in one of them. I graduated second in my class of about 450 students in January of 1961.

Since my parents didn't want me to attend a college far away from home, I had only three choices: Penn State, Temple and Penn. Penn was my first choice, because I wanted to meet people of different religions and cultures, people from all over the world.

There was only one full-paid scholarship at my high school, and it was to Penn. Fortunately for me, the boy who was first in our class didn't accept the scholarship; he wanted to go to a different school. I got the scholarship and was very happy.

My Penn Education
When I started at Penn, I didn't know what I wanted to do. My parents urged me to have some type of vocation, and they insisted I enroll in The School of Education. I knew I did not want to be a teacher. Fortunately for me, after one semester Penn abolished The School of Education and enrolled me in the College for Women (CW). I never took a teaching course.

I decided to be a math major, because I had done really well in math and science in high school. I had three semesters of calculus. Then, one of the professors who was on a sabbatical came back to Penn and I was enrolled in his class for set theory. It was the first time I ever had a problem in a math class, so I dropped it. Meanwhile, I had taken several chemistry classes and did well, so I switched my major to organic chemistry.

I recall taking one graduate course at the Moore School of Electrical Engineering. The class was numbers theory used in computers. I really liked that class. At the time, there was no computer science class or major.

I graduated from Penn with a degree in organic chemistry. My professor offered to help me get into graduate school but I declined his offer; I was burned out from studying.

Campus Life
I commuted to Penn the first semester. It still felt like high school, only the classes were a little harder. On a fraternity weekend, I stayed in a friend's room in the dorm. After that weekend, I decided to live in the dorm.

Living in the dorm was great! I met so many wonderful and different people. I really didn't do many things other than have fun in the dorm and enjoy myself listening to music at Houston Hall. I was also on the business staff of the *Daily Pennsylvanian*, responsible for laying out the paper. Besides my chemistry classes and being in CW, another aspect of college I loved and really enjoyed was the arts classes, especially History of the Symphony and three History of Art courses. My one regret is not joining a sorority.

Looking Back on my Penn Experience
Penn is a highly regarded school. My Penn degree was very valuable when I went to work at IBM and then as a consultant to MBNA.

My problem was I didn't set enough goals for myself. My initial goal was to get into Penn, but then I didn't set any other goals. Most of the students in my chemistry classes were guys, and a lot of them were pre-med. We would study together. Looking back, I should have gone to medical school; I would have made it.

My Career Begins
Penn provided excellent training in chemistry. When I worked as a chemist for nine months, all my chemistry classes gave me an excellent background. The only computer course at Penn in the electrical engineering school provided the basics which I used at IBM. IBM offered training in technical and leadership skills. I always got an interesting job at IBM. My bosses felt I did well and could handle the job.

IBM offered me a "job" nine months after I graduated from Penn. At the time, I had been working as a chemist, but my heart was no longer in chemistry. Little did I know my IBM career would span 20 years, with more than five years working with international customers and European IBMers.

My "class" at IBM (front, second from left).

Actually, I had two "careers" with IBM—one while I was living in Cherry Hill, New Jersey, and the second in Dallas, Texas. The first part of my career at IBM was in the Trenton, N.J., office and then in Philadelphia. Shortly after I joined IBM, I contracted hepatitis. My doctor told me the commute to Trenton was too long. I was able to swap positions with a woman who preferred Trenton, and I went to Philadelphia where I was a Systems Engineer. The sales people sold the computer equipment; I was responsible for programming and installing the product to meet the customer's needs.

Although my interest was in being assigned to the petro-chemicals group, I was assigned to the distribution office. I progressed through the ranks but remained a Systems Engineer in the wholesale and retail sales division. One of our clients was Food Fair Stores. That's where I met my husband.

When point of sale (POS) systems were becoming popular, I very much wanted to join that group. IBM did not allow me to be a part of that group because I was pregnant at the time. I took a leave of absence for eight weeks to have my son, and then decided to retire from IBM. .

My Return to IBM—The Career Journey Continues
My husband changed his job, and we moved to Dallas. A good friend of mine in Dallas told me IBM was looking for someone part-time to be a liaison between IBM and a company in California that was documenting programs for the Dallas office. I interviewed and took the job offer. After 18 months, IBM advised me I could no longer work part-time. I went to work full-time in Dallas and stayed there another 11-plus years.

At IBM, I continued to move through the ranks and was put in charge of the highest level of customer support. When a customer called and no one else could assist them, the call came to my team.

Then I began to work internationally. For three years, I was a manager in a software development group responsible for the drop-down menus, help text and dictionaries for *Display Write*, a word processing system. We wrote the text and the manuals which had to be translated into different languages.

Most of the translators came from IBM Europe — France, Denmark, Sweden, Germany and Italy. Every time we released a new product, experts from these countries would come to our office, do the translations and test the translated product with the language dictionary to be certain it worked. I really loved working with the people from the different countries, and I credit Penn and all the History of Art courses for my love of different cultures.

Subsequently, I was promoted to project manager in the business office responsible for *Office Vision*. This group was charged with porting the *Office Vision* product from the IBM mainframe to the PC. A short time later I was offered a job as a product manager for PC Office Systems for Europe. Although this group was headquartered in Paris, my team continued to be based in the Dallas area. We analyzed sales and met with people from different countries in Europe to determine their software requirements. Then we worked with the software development lab to develop the software programs. In addition to the countries we worked with for *Display Write* in Western Europe, we also worked with individuals from Portugal, Iceland, Norway and Switzerland.

I took many trips to Europe as the liaison between marketing in Europe and the Software Development lab in Dallas. It was truly enjoyable going to and working with the people from Europe. My group would meet with the customers to make presentations and obtain feedback on our work product. To this day, I keep in touch with several individuals in Europe whom I met and worked with in those five years.

I didn't have a career path going into Penn nor did I have one at graduation, but I did very well. I worked with great people from IBM Europe and managed a $60MM product.

My 20-Year IBM Career Ends and a New Door Opens

When I retired from IBM, I had planned to go home, sit outside, play tennis, go out for coffee with my husband in the morning, etc. After six months, boredom set in and I started looking for another job.

Eventually I was offered an hourly position with a consulting company, Cutler Williams (later known as COMSYS), because the person who interviewed me was a former IBMer and he said, "I know you can do the job. It is programming and you worked at IBM. I can tell what kind of person you are."

My main account was MBNA, the credit card company. Everything I had learned at IBM as a Systems Engineer came back.

I began as a programmer at MBNA and eventually became a Systems Analyst, in charge of many projects. MBNA kept offering me a full-time job, but they could offer only benefits, not a significantly higher salary. Since I still had benefits from IBM, I never took the full-time offer. I was making more money being paid by the hour.

Although I worked with MBNA/COMSYS for 10 years, I didn't consider that a career.

In 2004, at 61 years of age I finally retired, but it was really hard at first to stop working, hard not to go into work. It took me a long time to adjust. My husband said I defined myself by my meetings.

My husband passed away in 2007. In the meantime, we had moved from our house to a high rise.

After my husband passed away, my grandchildren in New Jersey saw me a lot. Volunteering at Scottish Rite Hospital, similar to Shriners Hospital, filled the hours in my day and was very rewarding. I volunteered for nearly four years until back problems and surgery ended my volunteer efforts.

Now, I'm on the board and secretary of our condo association. I also play bridge a couple times a week.

The Women's Challenge

Being a woman never got in my way. I had two careers at IBM: before my son was born and after. IBM didn't hold it against me that I took a leave of absence after my maternity leave ended. If IBM had allowed me to work on the POS system, I would have returned after my son was born.

IBM really did not have a problem with women's career advancement when I returned the second time. In Philadelphia, women were not advancing so much, but eight years later in Dallas, there was a career path. I did well in my performance reviews and was happy with my raises. When I retired from IBM in 1993, I was making $75,000 a year, which I thought was good.

Passing on the Experience

I regret I did not go back to Penn to talk with students about the challenges of my career, and what I wished I might have done. I know there were no precedents to follow, no women CEOs we could relate to at that time, and the big women's movement hadn't started in the mid-1960s.

Thinking back now, I realize we were pioneers. I'm hoping this book can offer some valuable lessons to women just starting out today.

My son, daughter-in-law and grandchildren.

CONSTANCE HORNER

AN ENGLISH MAJOR BECOMES A
U.S. GOVERNMENT LEADER

Women today are leading in the practice of law, business, medicine, the arts, the ministry, government and more. Much of it has happened in the slightly more than the 50 years since I graduated from Penn. I and my classmates from 1964 came away from our university experience with confidence and energy before there were wide-spread movements that created a frame for advancement. Success in our era was individually driven. In spite of a lot of cultural change, it still is.

Constance McNeely Horner

My Early Years

The self-confidence which spoken and written command of the English language generates has played an important role in my professional and, therefore, personal life to this very day. For this, I thank the Sisters of Christian Charity, for their teaching; my mother, for whom correct speech was a necessary virtue and important social identifier; my Nanny (grandmother), who came every day to help out and sang nursery rhymes all day; and the genetic gods for blessing me with a powerful language-attainment gene.

I grew up in an Irish Catholic family in Chatham, a small town in northern New Jersey. My father taught high school biology and chemistry in the next town over. My mother was at home, taking care of me and my three brothers and my sister. I was fortunate to find school work an easy pleasure in my parochial elementary school and at Chatham's public high school. Reading and writing became a small passion which gave me SAT scores that got me into Penn and which stood me in good stead later on in the Federal government policy and political roles I assumed, as well as in my years of teaching.

The mother of one of my high school classmates urged me to apply to Smith College, which I did and to which I was accepted with a full scholarship. I also was accepted to Sarah Lawrence College with a full scholarship. Both of these schools were all-women at the time. My mother and I also visited Boston College, a Catholic college, but my recollection is that she and my father were fairly neutral in communicating to me on what basis I should choose a school.

Choosing Penn
Then I visited Penn. I loved it immediately, applied, and was offered a full and generous room, board, and tuition scholarship (the Benjamin Franklin Scholarship). My parents had given me no indication they had a preference. Much later, I found out my father had wanted me to go to Smith, but he kept it to himself.

When I visited the Penn campus, then as now it exuded intellectual and social vitality. It was an opening up of life for me. There were nearby churches with free concerts on Sunday afternoons. There were flyers announcing interesting people who would be coming to lecture. There was the whole city a short walk away. Not to put too fine a point on it, there also were men — three for each woman admitted, if memory serves. After a very studious and diligent high school experience, I wanted to go out and have some fun.

Financial aid was a great gift. We weren't expected to have loans and I had none when I graduated. To earn extra money, I worked in the women's dorm at the New Residence Hall (now Hill House) as a waitress. I waited on my peers, but that didn't bother me.

Defining a Career Path
I had no expectation of having a career. I believed I would become a high school English teacher until I married or until I had children and that would be the full limit of my work life outside the home. Yet I began to realize a huge ambition for life, for the world, for getting out there, for doing things, for seeing things. But I expected then to realize all of that through my choice of husband.

I had a lively interest in political theory and in English literature. For the love of reading, as well as for practical reasons, English became my major. It would allow me to get the high school teaching job I had to have right away upon graduation in order to earn a living. I might have majored in political science, except that I couldn't see it leading to a high school teaching job. Graduate school would have been nice, but I had no money, only a fledgling ambition.

Someone suggested that I might gain some perspective if I spoke with Dean Jean Brownlee, a very wise woman who cared a lot for us callow undergraduates. She asked me, "Where do you see yourself five years from now?" My response was that I would like to see myself among people who shaped things, who were very actively engaged in the world. She said, "Well, then you better go to graduate school." When I left the meeting, I said to myself, "But I can't go to graduate school." But the seed had been planted, to grow later on.

I met my husband, Charles Horner, also class of '64, at Penn. He became a profound influence in catapulting me into achieving ambitions on my own, not just through someone else. He was, and still is to this day, extremely supportive of me, encouraging me, confident in me in ways which I find to be incredible. He was a writer for the *Daily Pennsylvanian* when I first encountered him briefly freshman year, when I was among the first four women to "heel" the *Daily Pennsylvanian*. We met again at Activities Night in our junior year and began a life-long friendship, comprised in large part of a perpetual, ongoing schmooze about events large and small.

My grades shot up after Charles injected some discipline into my studies (as opposed to my raging extracurricular, sorority, and other social life). Looking back, though, I can say without doubt my leadership experience started in all those extracurricular activities at Penn. They were massively consequential for me in learning how to lead. I ran for President of the Women's Student Government (WSG) and won, not without a lot of help from favorable campaign coverage by the *Daily Pennsylvanian*.

Each evening during the campaign, Charles and I would go out for coffee and cigarettes to the Chuck Wagon on (I think) 41st and Chestnut Streets to talk about ideas to propose.

I was critical of the status quo and wanted to inject new ideas into campus governance. This orientation was part of the cultural shift going on at Penn and other universities at the time. The expectation of an orderly process of elevating to the WSG Presidency someone who had paid her dues in a vice-presidential role was ripe for disruption. I had had less experience than my competition, but I came out strongly with new ideas, and I won quite resoundingly by emphasizing a desire for innovation and change and a

Our wedding photo

confrontation with the then-current administration. My opponent would doubtless have won in the old context of campus politics. We weren't yet in what became known later on as "the Sixties." But we were at the beginning.

The political lessons I learned at Penn through extracurricular activities have stayed with me throughout my life. I've thought from time to time about how much energy I devoted to extracurricular activities rather than very valuable studies. If I could do it all over, I'd have studied more and run around somewhat less. But, really, it was worth it.

Charles and I eloped to Penn Chaplain Stanley Johnson a year after graduation. We were married in his office in the Student Union. Happy days!

Following An Independent Path

I've had have a lifetime love of literature. My general liberal arts education turned out to be extraordinarily valuable in my later government work. By constant reading of works of literature, history, philosophy, and politics at Penn and then for an M.A. at the University of Chicago, I came to understand a great deal about human nature. This is a source of life satisfaction. It has also been of practical value. For example, during my career in government, this understanding was immensely helpful in negotiating with cabinet secretaries over their budgets, and congressmen and senators over laws and regulations. I saw patterns I could recognize right away. I could understand and respond to quite subtle signs of character and belief, of feeling and thinking. I had already "read all about it," so to speak.

Following graduation from Penn, I was basically on my own. I could not afford to go to graduate school, and I also could not afford to live without a job. There was no networking to turn to. I didn't know any people, and Penn, as far as I could tell, offered no help. I had four siblings coming up behind me whom my parents would need to support. My solution was to go to the New York State Employment Office in Manhattan and say, "I just graduated from college. I need a teaching job." They sent me out to East Islip High School in Long Island, where I was hired to teach ninth and tenth grade English for $5,200 a year.

At the end of that year, Charles and I got married and moved to Chicago, where he began graduate studies in Asian history at the University of Chicago. The first year there, I commuted from Hyde Park to Oak Park, to teach English at its high school.

Graduate School and a Move Abroad

The following year I was admitted to the M.A. program at Chicago in English Literature, thanks in part to our decision to borrow the money and to some surprisingly nice letters of recommendation from several Penn professors. I loved the history of religion, having had an excellent introductory course at Penn, and had applied also to the University of Chicago Divinity School the same year that I applied for the English

Literature graduate program. Although I was accepted in both, I chose English Literature because the Divinity School requirements were so onerous that I could not see spending my prime childbearing years with no money while studying ancient languages.

After I received my M.A., I was accepted into the PhD program at Chicago in English Literature, but the department turned down my application for a fellowship even though my grades were strong. So I just thought, "Well, that's it; I can't go." But Charles said, "Oh, yes, you can. Go to the chairman of the department and make the case that you deserve a fellowship." I was intimidated by the prospect of the encounter, but I went in. The chairman was visibly unhappy to see me. He said to me, "You know, you're going to have a baby and you're not going to finish your program so why should we invest in you? You're not going to finish your PhD." I persisted and was granted a fellowship. But, ironically, a month or so later, Charles received a National Defense Education Act grant to spend two years in the Far East studying Chinese and Japanese, in Taipei and Tokyo. So, I went with him.

While he studied, I taught. What an adventure! I taught English composition to Chinese graduate students at Taiwan Normal University and the National Political Science University. I taught the Taipei City Planning Council spoken English on their lunch hour. I taught World Literature to soldiers at the American military base in Taipei in a course sponsored by an extension division of the University of Maryland. They were mostly very young African-American men from Appalachia. They were very proud to be taking their first college course. It was the best teaching job I ever had.

We had our first baby in Tokyo, in a Catholic hospital run by German nuns and Japanese doctors.

Soon after that we went to Washington for my husband's research and, eventually, my new part-time teaching job at a D.C. private high school. We had our second son at Georgetown University Hospital—a more culturally comfortable experience than the first.

Entering U.S. Government Service
In Washington I began to wonder about entering into the world beyond home and school, not as a big player, just as an observer actually. I wanted to see more of how the world worked. I was also developing a sense of mission that would lead me into politics and government. I was interested in learning how the political world worked, seeing it and observing human nature in this milieu. That and my mission for change in American public policy and culture were my motives. That mission

would lead me away from the Democratic Party in which I was reared and educated, to become a Reagan Republican.

I didn't know if I had the necessary capabilities for entry into that world, but my husband's encouragement and some of his relationships helped a great deal in getting me over the initial hurdles.

Getting the scholarship to Penn, as well as my parents' belief in me, had given me intellectual confidence. When I would have periods of self-doubt, which everyone has, my husband's reassurance was vital. Sheryl Sandburg said in *Lean In* that the most important career decision a woman can make is to pick the right life partner (aka husband). I agree with that.

My entry into a U.S. Government appointment had its beginnings in the 1979-80 campaigns, first in the primaries for George H. W. Bush and then in the national Reagan/Bush campaign. The only time-slot and activity available to me at Reagan's national campaign headquarters was as a volunteer during the hours of midnight to 7 a.m. My task was to produce overnight a report on press coverage of the previous day's world and political events, to

Charles and Connie

be faxed at 7 a.m. to the traveling campaign planes. Then I would go home and get my two boys off to school; sleep for five or six hours; go pick them up; and then at 11 p.m. drive from the District of Columbia, where we lived, across the Potomac River into Virginia to campaign headquarters.

When Reagan won, Charles and I both went into the Reagan and Bush Administrations as political appointees. I was so naïve that I didn't even know that campaign volunteers might have this opportunity.

94

For my first job in government, I was offered a salary level that seemed to be on the low side. Charles didn't want me to accept it. He insisted, "You have to argue for higher pay to start because where you start may influence where you end up. You have to be put into the Senior Executive Service on day one." Of course, it was unsettling to me to make this demand. I

didn't want to get this new boss mad. What if he said, "No" and we had a bad relationship? But I was more concerned about disappointing my husband's expectations. Believing in his judgment, I went to see the head of the agency and, rather begrudgingly, he said

To Constance Horner — With Best Wishes
Ronald Reagan

if he had to, he'd do it. Happily, he did.

I served in six different, progressively more responsible appointments in the twelve years of Presidents Reagan and Bush. In every case, men I

knew supported me for those positions, men who were advisers to the political sphere or who were in charge. The only time I lost out (to be Secretary of Labor), an exceedingly capable woman was appointed.

In the Oval Office with President Bush

My presidential appointments were: Director of VISTA; Associate Director of the White House Office of Management and Budget; Director of the U.S. Office of Personnel Management; Deputy Secretary of the Department of Health and Human Services; and White House Assistant to President Bush and Head of Presidential Personnel. I later served on the U.S. Commission on Civil Rights.

After Administration service, I took a position as Guest Scholar at the Brookings Institution to write and lecture on public sector management reforms. I also taught a few courses as a "practice professor" of government at Princeton University and Johns Hopkins University. Since that time, I've had the good fortune to be invited to serve on several public company boards of directors, including Pfizer, Prudential Financial, and Ingersoll Rand.

Fulfilling a Board Member's Role

I've never encountered much of a barrier as a woman. Like many women who were invited to join corporate boards as the trend grew in my era, I came out of government and academia, while male members were mostly CEOs of corporations. In that era, few women had the requisite CEO-level business experience. That's not true anymore. My opinions may have been somewhat discounted in occasional boardroom discussions because I didn't have a business background. When the subject was a government-related issue, however, my views were respected. A good board will have a variety of backgrounds and experiences reflected in its composition.

In the 1990s, when women started to be brought on to corporate boards with some regularity, it was considered a highly valued attainment. I went sideways from high-ranking government to high-ranking boards. I know that rising is an entirely different story for women who come up through an organization's ranks.

Social Intelligence, Self-Confidence, Close Relationships

For today's women getting their education at Penn or other institutions, and for those already functioning in the business and professional worlds, here are some of my observations from nearly a half-century of experiences in the public and private sectors.

- Personal drive and social intelligence are key. Penn played a huge part in my own social intelligence development.

- Conveyed self-confidence molds others' opinions of you. But a little good-natured self-deprecation is a sign of self-awareness that people appreciate.

- Close observation of the habits of others provides insight into what facilitates their performance under stress. During the October 1962 Cuban Missile Crisis, my sorority sisters played non-stop bridge to relieve the tension of the situation by focusing on their game. Later on, I came to understand why many CEOs play golf; it allows them to focus on the game to the exclusion, for a few hours, of fear, worry, and critical business concerns.

• A show of warmth toward others and casual conversation facilitate understanding. At Penn, I intuitively learned social understanding through engaging with those around me, especially in active participation with fellow students in extracurricular activities.

• Teachers and mentors can help you activate your particular talents, but "networking" too much can suggest that social relationships are merely for practical purposes. It's good to have real friends.

• Finally, it matters in life and work to have a broad mission. Self-advancement, in itself, is not a worthy mission. Spiritual or social purpose can offer validation in times of failure — and make success all the more sweet.

Being piped aboard the aircraft carrier USS Kitty Hawk at the Philadelphia Naval Shipyard for its 20-year overhaul. Piping aboard is a welcoming ceremony to honor visiting government officials. At the time, I was Director of the U.S. Office of Personnel.

MARION HUBING, ESQ.

DUAL CAREERS IN CHEMICAL ENGINEERING AND LAW

I found, throughout my career, that getting along with people was as important, if not more so, than being competent in your field of work. Politics, especially in big companies, played a heavy role with respect to promotions and it still does. It often depended upon whom you knew, not always what you knew.

Marion Sokal Hubing

My Early Years

When I was growing up in Philadelphia, I played with dolls like other little girls but was far more interested in experimenting with my chemistry set. Math and science were fascinating to me. I went to Philadelphia High School for Girls. It and Central High School for Boys were the top scholastic high schools in the city. I was number six in my class of 75, which carried with it a full tuition scholarship to Penn. I chose to pursue chemical engineering. I knew I'd probably be the only female student in the program, and I was. (Actually, one or two other girls started with me, but I was the only one to graduate with the class.)

There wasn't outside encouragement for me to study engineering. My encouragement basically came from the books I read about careers that could be open to me with training in math, science, and engineering. Originally, my parents were planning to send me to Temple University because they could not afford Penn. My first choice was MIT, but they didn't offer a scholarship, so my father made the choice for me. "There's no way we can afford MIT; you're going to take the scholarship to Penn." For the first semester I had to commute from my parents' house in the West Oak Lane section of Philadelphia. It took two hours out of my day, every day. I knew with my course workload I had to live on campus if I were to get the grades needed to keep my scholarship.

Dean Arthur Humphrey was my first advisor at Penn, followed by Dr. Mitchell Litt. Both were wonderful. For example, when the male chemical engineering students got summer jobs working in the refineries, and I did not, these two professors created a job for me in the Penn Engineering Department.

I met my husband at Penn during my freshman year. He was a student at Penn Law School at that time. He also was in the Army Reserve. His reserve unit was activated as a result of the Berlin crisis in 1961. We decided to marry so I could visit him in Germany.

I graduated in 1964 with a Bachelor of Science degree in Chemical Engineering, the same year the Civil Rights Act passed. Of about 18 students who received our degrees, I finished second from the top. As a woman, I couldn't officially be a member of the Penn chapter of Tau Beta Pi, the engineering honor society. Instead, I was made an honorary member and went to the meetings like all the guys did but I didn't have to pay any dues. My grades were good all throughout undergraduate school, and I received a number of awards, including: the American Chemist Society Award; the American Society for Testing Materials (ASTM) Award and membership in Pi Mu Epsilon, the mathematics honor society. My brother, Allen Sokal, graduated four years after me, also from Penn in chemical engineering.

Penn did a very good job to attract companies to conduct student interviews on campus. My first job in engineering, and later a job after I finished law school in 1990, came from on-campus interviews.

Interview Questions and Job Offers
The questions I was asked at the job interviews for chemical engineers wouldn't be tolerated today. When I sat down for one on-campus interview, the interviewer from Atlantic Refining Company (ARCO) said to me, "Let me be frank. We don't have facilities for women at any of our refineries." Then, I was asked during other interviews, "Are you married? When do you plan to have children?" Another big question was, "Do you think it's fair that we spend all this money training you when you start? You might have graduated as an engineer but there's a lot of on-the-job training. Then after we've invested all this money training you, you decide to have children and stay home." The interviewers, were, of course, male.

My engineering professors were concerned I wasn't getting job offers following the interviews, as were the men in my class. They decided to put in a good word for me, as I was to graduate *Magna Cum Laude* in engineering. Their strategy was to take the interviewers out to lunch and talk me up as an outstanding engineering student who could make a valuable contribution to their company. That helped. Thanks to them, I got two offers, one from the chemical company Rohm and Haas. There were always barriers, but at Penn I was lucky there also were always allies.

Before I graduated, I entertained the idea of continuing my education to earn a PhD in engineering. I thought a PhD would be important if I decided to go into research. I applied for the PhD program at Princeton University. When they turned me down, I was told it was because they didn't accept women in that program. One of the Penn professors knew the Princeton dean of engineering, and he said, "Let me talk to my contact and tell him what an exception you are," but it didn't work. He came back to me and said, "Look, he won't do it, but if you still want to get a PhD, we can offer you a total fellowship at Penn." I gave it some thought, but thanked him and didn't take him up on it. Instead, I thought I would work and earn some money.

Programming Computers in a Male Environment

I went to work at Rohm and Haas (R&H) in the Central Engineering Department on Process Control. That was at the very beginning stages when we were designing and programming computers to be used in the running of chemical plants. This was very new technology, and I was excited to be working on it. We were a team of three: my boss, another chemical engineer and me. I had been married since the beginning of my sophomore year at Penn. For plant start-up, I was stationed in Deer Park, Texas for three months. That was a new experience for me, being away from home for that long a period.

In the control house where the instrumentation for the plant was located, there was a single bathroom that lacked a door. There were no facilities at all for women, except at the main business office, near the front gate of the site, about a mile away. So when I had to use the ladies room, I'd hop in the car and drive to the office building (think *Hidden Figures*).

I worked at R&H for three years as a chemical engineer focusing on the process control of a new methanol plant. I stayed there until I had my first baby, a boy named Richard in 1967. In the third month of my pregnancy, I started showing. I was approached by my boss (the lead engineer on the process control project) and was told, "Personnel has advised me that it's inappropriate for a woman to work when she starts to show." All along, I had thought that R&H was a progressive company on such matters and would be very understanding. Well, they weren't. I had no choice in the matter. They told me, "Sorry, goodbye. Come back after the baby is born."

Balancing a 20-year Career at Sun Oil Co.

While I was on unpaid maternity leave from R&H, I decided to apply for a job at Sun Oil Company. At the job interview, Sun Oil Company indicated I would not meet the same biased fate that marked my involuntary leave of absence from R&H. Policies at Sun Oil did indeed seem more liberal. They hired me when I was an expectant mother. I was

very open with them about my future family plans. "I hope I can work until shortly before I give birth. I don't want to be forced out. And, I plan to have other children," I told them. "Oh, no problem here," they said. I accepted a job at Sun Oil as a process engineer and worked there for 20 years.

However, their outlook on maternity leave was inconsistent. I started working at Sun Oil in 1967, shortly after my son, Richard, was born. When I was hired by Sun, the deal was that I wouldn't have to leave until I was ready to leave and could come back two weeks after the baby was born. But in 1968, before my daughter, Esther, was born, I was called into the office of the HR director who said to me, "We're sorry, but HR is concerned about insurance liability. After the end of your fifth month you're going to have to leave." So I was forced into another unpaid leave of absence.

Back at Sun
My first assignment was in the computer section of Sun's Central Engineering Department. We wrote the computer programs in Fortran to design distillation columns and heat exchangers as well as programs to simulate refinery process flow. My true objective was to work at the refinery and do what I call, "hands-on dirty work." But there was no way, as a woman, I could get a job like that in the company. They wouldn't allow it. "Girls" didn't do those things." The only time I worked in the refinery was during a strike in 1984; they let me go into the Sun Oil Marcus Hook refinery. My job was dock duty with the

supervisors to bring in the ships — the crude oil tankers and the barges. That was a real team effort; I loved it. For me, it was almost as much fun as being in summer camp.

When I was doing technical design, I applied mathematical equations I had learned at Penn. For example, when designing a distillation column, I had to determine how many distillation plates to put in the column to meet the desired product specifications.

There were other assignments, not so demanding. Corporate management put me on a special task force, which was a task force of one — me. It had absolutely nothing to do with engineering. My assignment was to interview all of the executives and ask them if they felt the company should or should not keep our corporate aircraft. The question was whether we should we get rid of them and make everyone fly on commercial airlines. You can imagine the responses. They came up with every kind of reasoning you could think of to keep the corporate planes. "Oh," they would tell me, "when we go to Europe for a negotiation, it's far more productive for us, and we're rested and refreshed having flown on our company's plane." They wanted to make sure I agreed the corporate aircraft should stay. Of course I wrote a report that said it should. Anything negative would have been unacceptable.

For the most part, the people I worked with in middle management were fair and unbiased, except for the last boss. He was from Colombia, and he really resented my presence as a woman in his section. He assigned a project to me that I knew was mathematically impossible to do. My explanation to him of why it wasn't solvable the way he wanted it was to no avail. "I don't care; you do it," he said. There was no solution that could be applied to produce the result he specified. A short time later, he laid me off.

There was nothing I could do about it. A close friend in HR, Judy Hutchinson, couldn't contradict the termination. She and her lawyer husband, Jim, who also was at Sun in the legal department, suggested I take a voluntary severance package and accept Sun's offer to go to law school, tuition-free. Sun made arrangements for the final financial payment, and I went to law school at Penn. Becoming an attorney had never been in my focus as a career objective. Looking back over 20 years of working as a chemical engineer, and evaluating what I did and did not accomplish, I was disappointed. The reasons for my lack of advancement had nothing to do with my qualifications as a chemical engineer. Rather, they were more about my status as a woman engineering professional in the company. I regret not having more chances to get my hands dirty.

The Women United

At Sun Oil, a group of women got together and filed a class action suit against the company for discrimination, citing a lack of advancement, which was true. In my case, I wanted so much to be a manager of a group of engineers. In the computer department, I did become a manager and had five people working in my section. But once I was transferred back to the engineering department, my title was staff engineer. I never made it to a manager level, even though I had the necessary qualifications. Men who used to work for me in the computer department would be promoted to managers, but I was repeatedly bypassed. I saw that happening all the time.

There was one instance where I was offered a promotion as a group manager. It meant transferring to Toledo, Ohio, where Sun Oil operated a refinery. There was no way I could go. My husband was practicing law in Philadelphia and was not a member of the Ohio bar. In retrospect, my analysis of that offer is that management knew I couldn't accept the job, but they could have it on the books that I turned down a promotion, and they didn't need to elaborate on the reason in writing.

It made me pose the question to myself: "Was it because I'm a woman or is it because there's something wrong with me?" No one at Sun Oil would tell you, "It's because you're a woman." I did not have any self-confidence when I worked as an engineer. I was shy…not sure of myself. The lack of promotions made me feel I was inadequate.

I decided I had to switch careers at age 43 and become an attorney. Law was always in the family, and my husband encouraged me to go to law school when I got laid off. He said, "You're the only one in your family who's not a lawyer. Both your cousin, Ingrid, and your brother are lawyers. You are the only non-lawyer. Here's your opportunity. Go for it."

At Penn law school, there were female professors, and at least 30 percent of the student body was women. Law school is where I gained my self-confidence. Everyone admired me in law school. With the age gap, I could have been the mother to the other students. The professors liked me, and my fellow students treated me wonderfully. That's where I really got my confidence.

Almost all students joined a study group of 4 to 6 students, in which they divided the work among themselves for outlining each course. My study groups usually met at my house in Valley Forge, although it was quite a distance from Penn's campus. My husband would cook lunch or dinner, so maybe that is why they preferred to meet at my house. It made me feel I really belonged and was accepted. I also was invited to many parties given by the students.

After I graduated from Penn with a J.D. degree (*Magna Cum Laude*), I worked at Dechert Price and Rhoads in Philadelphia for about two years as an associate. I did mostly transactional work and felt like a glorified paper shuffler. I interviewed with White and Williams, also in Philadelphia, to be part of their reinsurance litigation group (reinsurance is insurance for

insurance companies). We did what is called litigation risk analysis. It involves a lot of math and was a perfect fit for me, because I used my math background. Math is scary to a lot of lawyers.

I really enjoyed my job at White and Williams. There was no discrimination. My boss was a female until I retired at the end of 2010 at age 68. The only reason I retired was because my husband was so ill. It was up to me to take care of him. After he passed away, White and Williams called and asked if I wanted to come back. I very much appreciated their reaching out to me, but I was unable to accept. I was too burned out at that point. Also, I loved retirement as I could play tennis every day, audit courses and continue my activities as a member of the alumni boards of the engineering and law schools at Penn.

Penn asked me several times to participate in panel discussions about careers but not specific to the engineering school. The Philadelphia public schools invited me to talk to students about career opportunities in engineering, the sciences, and law.

Me, second from left.

I never stayed home except when I was forced to for a few months. Several of my friends chose to stay at home until their children were old enough to start school and then they went back to work. They were teachers. There was really no advancement in that profession unless you became a principal.

The most successful engineers I came in contact with had good communication skills. If the head of the department became out of favor, then the whole department suffered.

I've kept up my memberships in several professional societies. At Penn, I am still very active, including the Association of Alumnae. I'm a member of the board of directors of the law school and the engineering school, and I was the first female president of the Engineering Alumni Society (making me a lifetime member of the board). Both my daughter and I serve on the board of the Penn law school alumni association, making us one of the few, if not the only, mother-daughter combination board members of a major law school alumni association in the U.S.

NEEN HUNT

A DIVERSIFIED CAREER
AND WORLD TRAVELER

In high school, I wanted to be involved in every type of activity. I wanted to experience it all. Every day I try to keep learning, meet different people, continue to travel, and broaden my experiences so that my world is continually evolving. I have always wanted to "grab life by the horns" and ride it into challenging territories.

My intellectual life and journey began at Penn. I am so proud to have been one of the women, among 385 others, to be in the first large class of freshmen women at Penn in 1960. Learning and living in the midst of 4,000 undergraduate male students, we were privileged to experience an extraordinary time. To the women who are yet to enter this exceptional institution, I would offer this thought: Bloom where you are planted; this garden is rich and fertile.

Neen (Esther) Schwartz Hunt

My Early Years
I was educated entirely by the Upper Darby public school system, located beyond the Philadelphia, Pa., city line. I lived in a working class neighborhood inhabited predominantly by Italian Catholics. Neither of my parents was college educated. My mother was a high school graduate but my father dropped out of school in seventh grade. In my high school of nearly 1,000 students, I was selected to be in the academic track. Most of the girls in my high school, even in the advance placement classes, did not seem to have college aspirations. It seemed to me securing a job at the local Woolworth defined success, as did getting married. I always knew I wanted to live beyond the boundary of my neighborhood. I dreamed of working for National Geographic or, at the very least, marrying an explorer who would take me around the globe.

My father was a taxi driver and my mother worked as a saleswoman. With three girls in the family, I had to earn spending money. As I grew older, I worked at various part-time jobs, such as at a bagel shop and the local pancake house on weekends and during the summers. These experiences taught me many lessons about succeeding in the work place, dealing with a boss and appreciating how hard it is to earn money. As a young girl, I also launched my sustained, deep interest in the creative arts by writing a weekly neighborhood newsletter that included a fiction series, writing a horror story and writing and performing plays for the neighbors that, in retrospect, were variations on the story of Romeo and Juliet.

During my junior year in high school, I had a very supportive college counselor who guided me through the application process and was responsible in part for my acceptance to Penn. When we began the college search, my mother had encouraged me to become a teacher and to attend West Chester State Teachers' College. As it turned out, Penn gave me the most generous scholarship. When I hesitated about this decision (I was worried I could not compete with other Penn students), my parents were emphatic that I had to attend Penn because they believed it was a world class institution.

Perhaps my mother, who died at age 50 a few years after I had graduated from Penn, was the greatest influence on my education. She had many artistic talents, and for a few years she owned and managed a small clothing shop, Sarah L. Schwartz Distinctive Fashions. She had ambitions for her daughters and my expectations for my own life were very much shaped by her standards and values. Like many Jewish families, learning was always important in our home and evening discussions touched on current events, politics, history, entertainment and people who were making a difference in the world. Being an excellent student, I read constantly and always seemed to have "my head in a book." I loved reading fiction like the Nancy Drew series, but I also read to gain information. I remember reading *Popular Science* and *Popular Mechanics* — my father's favorite magazines — to learn how things work. I was inquisitive during an age when girls were not encouraged to be scholars but rather to be secretaries, nurses or teachers.

My Penn Education
I commuted each day on the subway to Penn for two years, and sometimes took advantage of offers to stay with other women who had their own apartments or with friends who were living at a sorority house. I know my parents struggled financially to pay the bills, but each year Penn increased the aid. During my final year, all expenses were paid, including living in the brand new girls' dormitory on 34th street. However, it was still stressful not to have the financial resources to take vacations, to buy trendy clothes and to socialize in clubs and at restaurants with my peers. I did not like sorority life because it reinforced cliques and the notion of "insiders and outsiders." Over the years at Penn, these memberships began to mean very little with respect to my relationships.

When I entered Penn, I thought I would become a child psychiatrist. I wanted to understand why intellectual capacities are so different, and why some are more valued than others.

During my first two years at Penn, I remained committed to becoming a doctor. One summer, I worked as a candy striper at the University of Pennsylvania Hospital in the neonatal unit. Then fate intervened and, in my sophomore year, my mother's small dress shop failed and went into bankruptcy. It was a traumatic family experience that taught me lessons about the personal costs of stress and failure, and the damage to self-image caused when so much of self-worth seems to be defined by financial success in our society.

I mentioned to my father, at the time, I still wanted to go to medical school. His reply was sobering: "I can't even pay for a microscope so I suggest you think about doing something else." Unfortunately, there weren't a lot of women who were in medicine then. Looking back, I think it was a mistake that I didn't seek out someone who could have advised me about obtaining scholarship money. Instead I changed my career direction.

For my remaining two years at Penn, I majored in English. I had confidence in my writing skills and, fortunately, I was influenced by Professor Turner who taught the Shakespeare course. Dr. Turner motivated me to improve my own abilities to express my thoughts in writing. He was an extraordinary teacher who deepened my appreciation and understanding of the power of literature to inform and educate. I learned from him that a talented teacher can impact young minds. He, most likely, affected my own decision to become a teacher as I pursued an occupation.

I credit Penn most with expanding my mind and preparing me for a career in journalism and education. As a Penn woman, I began to value my own intellect and to have confidence in my abilities. I wanted to learn more to increase my knowledge and deepen my understanding, rather than just to earn an A. My desire to know and to understand began to replace the importance I had placed on good grades. So many of the professors at Penn contributed to my intellectual growth. Russian History, the History of Art, 20th century Drama, 18th century poetry, Logic and Rhetoric, Experimental Psychology — each of these courses was taught by leading scholars who not only deepened my knowledge of these different fields but also excited my curiosity to learn more. I was in awe of the scholars at Penn and felt grateful to be taught by the very people who wrote the textbooks I was studying.

Penn professors also helped me relate to my own mind, as well as to come to terms with its limitations. I placed greater value on my intellectual strengths and began to realize their power to affect others. My experience as a student at Penn expanded my world, but it also made me a larger and more complex person. I credit Penn with helping me to appreciate my reasoning abilities and expanding my intellectual scope.

The professors at Penn raised provocative questions that opened my mind to new possibilities. In an environment that respected intellectual curiosity and allowed for debate, I thrived. I became interested in the big ideas that have shaped our civilization, and the large issues that confront our humanity and that advance civilization

Leadership and Personal Growth
I also benefited from the leadership roles that I was fortunate to experience at Penn. It was a privilege to be elected Freshman class President and Chief Justice of the Judiciary Board. I felt honored to have membership in the Mortarboard Society and Phi Beta Kappa. These affiliations offered me the opportunity to meet with incredible people like Loren Eiseley, the Provost of Penn but also a respected philosopher, anthropologist, and science writer. Experiences like this were life-changing.

Interestingly, when I look back on my leadership roles at Penn, I feel I did not take best advantage of these positions. At the time, I didn't seem to have an awareness of the kinds of changes that could improve a major institution like Penn, or how the women and men at Penn could be organized and galvanized to address issues in the larger society, such as poverty, racial discrimination and other injustices which were in plain sight in West Philadelphia.

During my years at Penn, I was eager to learn many subjects about which I knew very little. Growing up, I had never visited a museum or attended a live concert. My experiences at Penn awakened the part of myself that is an aesthete. I devoted myself to a marathon of reading great works of literature. Dostoyevsky and Hemingway became the focus for my senior thesis. Enrolled in the History of Music, I remember sitting in the music lab wearing headphones and listening for the first time to "The Rite of Spring" and "Bolero," as well as the breathtaking works of Bach, Rachmaninoff and Beethoven. I had never before heard classical music which since has helped to fill my life with beauty and imagination. Later in my life, I learned to play the flute, played in ensembles, and met accomplished musicians. I also had the good fortune to be elected to the Board of the Midori Foundation and to work with Midori herself, a generous and amiable individual whose brilliance and international success did not affect her ego. I realized at Penn how much I appreciate beauty, and especially the creative arts. Perhaps my adoration for the arts led me to fall in love with my husband of 40 years, a professional classical guitarist.

During my years at Penn, I don't think I had an insightful assessment of myself as a woman. As I remember it, the subject of gender, and its attendant benefits and disadvantages in our society, was not a topic of conversation or study. Although these were the Sixties, and women's rights was a new issue in the mainstream culture, I never thought of myself as a strong or "liberated" woman. I was keenly aware men dominated the world of work, and many occupations had raised barriers to hiring women. I didn't think about the fact that our society treated women so unequally. I was more inclined then to accept the status quo than to encourage change. Also, it surprises me to note that although I knew that I was in the first large class of women at Penn, I never realized its significance as a groundbreaking step for higher education.

My Career Begins

Graduating from Penn, I headed to New York City and a career in journalism. I landed a position with *School Library Journal*, writing reviews of young adult books and editing other book reviews. I lived with Ilene Leff, my former roommate at Penn, who also was working. I renewed my interest in working with young people, so I returned to school and entered the Master of Arts in Teaching Program at Harvard. I discovered I loved teaching and wanted to continue in this profession.

My International Career

At Harvard, I became good friends with a woman who had taught in Malawi, Africa, with the Crossroads Africa program. I joined Service to the People, a volunteer teaching program in Israel. As a Jew, and having been educated in Hebrew schools, I could read and write Hebrew, so I knew I could learn to speak the language which I eventually spoke fluently.

I was assigned to Kiriyat Gat, a new development in the southern Negev, and to a teaching position serving Bedouin children and recent immigrants from Iraq, Iran, Tunisia, Cyprus and Morocco. The classroom was at an agricultural training school located near the Bedouin camp. The living conditions were difficult. I taught over 50 students of all ages in one room. I made many friends who were Arabs, Israelis, Jews and non-Jews. I remained in the position for 15 months, at which time I was called home because my mother was seriously ill. I am so grateful I arrived in time to have a few months with her before she passed away from cancer.

Returning to my home to live with my father and to take care of my young sister, I worked for several years in public school teaching and in administrative positions in Philadelphia. During this time, I was recruited by ABT Associates, a consulting firm, to evaluate curricula on Indian reservations in Utah, in schools funded by the Bureau of Indian Affairs. For a year and a half, I lived at Intermountain School, a boarding school for Indian children. I travelled to many reservations throughout the west and was stunned by the poverty and ashamed at how our country has treated the Indian peoples. The families were plagued by alcoholism, divorce, mental illness, truancy and other problems typical of disadvantaged populations. Unfortunately, I don't believe my work had an impact on the schools at the sites I visited. The problems seemed intractable and in need of massive change, not easily influenced by my small contribution.

More Education at Harvard as My Career Evolves

When I returned home, I was accepted with a full scholarship into the doctoral program at the Harvard School of Education in a new program, Learning Environments. There were 13 other students. Because of my growth at Penn, I felt prepared for the Harvard experience and its competitive challenges. It took me five years to earn my doctorate and to complete a thesis analyzing the coping mechanisms of teachers in alternative school settings who were experiencing stresses related to moral and ethical conflicts.

The years living in Cambridge were eventful in so many ways. My very best friendships were formed there and I met my husband, who had recently returned from living for two years in Mexico to study with a master in classical guitar. My husband is a descendant of a high profile Boston family who came to America on the Mayflower. Many of his relatives are famous (including Richard Morris Hunt, the architect for the Newport mansions, the façade of the Metropolitan Museum of Art and the base of the Statue of Liberty). He was so different from men I had dated at Harvard. Light-heartened, artistic, optimistic about life, witty and a "true gentleman," William Morris Hunt III captured my heart. We married four years later. As newlyweds, we moved to New York City so Will could study with Manuel Barrueco, a preeminent Cuban classical guitarist. I commuted for a year from Cambridge until I secured employment at the Board of Education to oversee a project researching the school dropout problem.

Shortly thereafter, while eight months pregnant, I was selected to be the Head of the Calhoun School, a progressive K-12 co-ed private school of 600 students on the Upper West Side of Manhattan. I loved the work and remained in the position for 14 years, bearing two children along the

way. In my role as Head, I grew as an educator, manager and person. I deepened my knowledge of operations, budgets and investments, my skills as a public spokesperson, my abilities to resolve conflicts, and my confidence as a compelling leader. Under my leadership, Calhoun added a second campus on 74th street, built a library which now bears my name (I am so happy my father was alive to attend the ceremony), increased enrollment, diversified the student population, balanced budgets, strengthened the teaching faculty and administrative team, and increased the public profile of Calhoun as a successful  progressive school. Additionally, I was elected to more than several officer positions in state and national education organizations, which helped to burnish Calhoun's reputation.

The children of many powerful and prominent families were enrolled at Calhoun and, though it was challenging to deal with demanding parents, many of them and their children were wonderful people. Ben Stiller, Gabby Karan and Harper Simon were among the famous children. My meetings with Carly Simon and James Taylor, Robert DeNiro and Mick Jagger were memorable.

When we decided in 1993 as a family to move out of the city to Greenwich, Ct., I hesitated to resign but the commute was simply too far to manage. Soon thereafter, I was selected to be the superintendent of schools in New Canaan, Ct., a coveted positon that seemed too good to refuse. At the same time, however, I was recruited to assume a

With my grandchildren.

112

COO position with the United Nations Association, an advocacy and research program at the UN. This was a difficult decision. Over my husband's objection, I chose the UN position and commuted into New York for the next four years. I enjoyed the work, but was disappointed also. The job, unfortunately, was more administrative than substantive, and I didn't experience the global scale of work I had desired.

New Responsibilities and Experiences

As luck again would have it, I worked closely at UNA with a member of the finance committee, Christopher Brody, a managing partner at the investment firm of Warburg Pincus. Chris also was the grandson of Mary Lasker whose husband, Albert (known as the Father of American Advertising for his successes with Lucky Strike, White Rain, Xerox and other products) left her a fortune when he passed away. With the money, she started a foundation to support biomedical research to fulfill her goal to cure cancer. Today the Albert and Mary Lasker Foundation is internationally renowned for highlighting, honoring and rewarding seminal discoveries in basic and clinical research that have saved millions of lives, extended the lives of individuals all over the globe, and mitigated the pain and suffering of so many patients afflicted by disease and debilitated by serious injuries.

As a member of the Board of this private family foundation, Chris Brody invited me to become its CEO and President.

My role at the Foundation presented new professional challenges as well as exciting opportunities for personal growth. I discovered I was comfortable working with medical scientists and enjoyed learning about an entirely new field. I also augmented my skill set and took on new responsibilities, such as advocating for medical research at Congressional hearings and with government leaders. I thoroughly enjoyed working closely with politicians, and it was thrilling to meet many of the men and women who had devoted their lives to advancing the battle against disease and premature death: Jim Watson, the discoverer of DNA; Henry Heimlich, who developed the Heimlich Maneuver; Robert Edwards, who pioneered in vitro fertilization; and Dr. Michael DeBakey, the famed heart surgeon. They clearly were brilliant professionals but also engaging and delightful people. One year I attended the Nobel Prize ceremony in Stockholm to celebrate the award for research focused on deepening the understanding of Mad Cow disease that was presented to Stanley Pruisner (our Penn classmate), whom the Lasker Foundation had supported.

My experiences at Lasker taught me there are not enough women who are science professionals. I became more aware of the obstacles that women who want to pursue science careers often face, and especially the failure of schools to encourage and support young girls who have the talent and interest to work in science.

When my husband retired from his second career as the president of Coldwell Banker/Hunt Kennedy in Manhattan, we moved to Palm Beach Gardens, Florida. I had worked at the Lasker Foundation for 15 years

Presenting the Lasker Award for Public Service to Christopher Reeve, actor and chairman of the Christopher Reeve Paralysis Foundation, in 2003.

and I wanted to continue to work. I was hired as Special Advisor in the President's office at the Scripps Florida Research Institute, where I worked with the Board of Governors and the Development Office. Unfortunately, the work ended three years later when Richard Lerner, the President, retired.

In 2010, I was recruited by the billionaire Bill Koch to open a private high school in West Palm Beach, and hired as the Founding Head of School. It was a unique, exciting opportunity but, for a variety of reasons, I left the position after a year.

Without full-time work for the first time in my life, I continued my tutoring activities which I had begun in Greenwich. I have worked with hundreds of adults and students of all ages to prepare them for different standardized tests, to improve their writing, to help them think logically, and to learn in ways that deepen understanding. Additionally, I extended my reach as an educational consultant with a focus on training governing boards for nonprofit institutions, including schools, foundations and advocacy organizations. Now I present workshops for beginning and advanced governing boards and consult with school heads, executive directors, and senior executives to help them manage governing decisions and to settle conflicts.

Joining the Peace Corps
In 2015, at age 72, I was living in a high-end gated community in Florida. With a life of leisure, playing golf and tennis, and swimming and cycling, I decided to join the Peace Corps. I left a beautiful home, a loving husband and a secure lifestyle. Many people, including my

family, questioned this choice, especially when I was assigned to a tiny island, Pohnpei, in Micronesia, near the equator in the South Pacific. I made the choice because I wanted to continue to use my skills and knowledge to benefit people in need as long as I am able. I was hired to be a School Accreditation Specialist to prepare principals and teachers to meet the standards of the state accreditation process. I elected to live in the forest of Pohnpei in a tribal community.

My host family of 12 relatives, living in one room in a cement structure with a corrugated roof, was peaceful, generous and kind. The family provided me with a floor mattress while everyone else used a towel, and they made special food for me. Although the work was very challenging (so many people did not speak English and I had to be assisted by a translator), I believe that my skills and knowledge as an educator made a significant difference in the lives of principals and teachers in the six schools in which I worked. After 15 months on Pohnpei, I returned home via Asia, travelling for three weeks with Ilene Leff, my long time Penn friend.

Going Home and Looking Back

When I returned home in June 2016, I was engaged by the McCreight Strategy Implementation Consulting firm to assess the Ives School, located in Somers, N.Y., on the campus of Lincoln Hall, a residential facility for young men who have been assigned there by the juvenile court system. For the past six months as of this writing, I have been working with a team of eight other professionals to help the board of directors determine the future direction for this institution.

As a woman, there were barriers to professional success. In the senior executive positions I had held, I became keenly aware of the "old boys' network" and how important it was to know the "right people," most of whom were men. I became aware, too, of the wage gap between men and women, especially when I was a Head of School. At the same time, my style was not to confront or complain when I learned about unfair practices or policies related to gender differences and their impact on my own life. Rather, I worked hard to convince others of my special strengths and how I would be an asset. Despite some examples to the contrary I had witnessed, I continued to believe that merit and competence, above other considerations, would be recognized and rewarded. I think, too, that somewhat unconsciously I leveraged my identity as a woman, which then was more stereotypical than it seems to be today. I dressed well to appear feminine and attractive. I played the role of "peacemaker" when the men at the table were "locking horns." I injected levity and humor into serious deliberations to "crack the ice." I offered creative solutions when more practical alternatives appeared equally unappealing. I was conciliatory when others were "digging in their heels."

In these twilight years, I am grateful for my family and many friends all over the world. My eldest son, Evan, graduated Penn and the London School of Economics and, after 9/11, enlisted in the Air Force. After 29 missions to Iraq and Afghanistan, he is a Lieutenant Colonel who works in California for Raytheon on developing laser weapons. My second son, Richard, graduated Northeastern University and is a technology security risk analyst, having worked at PricewaterhouseCoopers, the Royal Bank of Scotland and GE Digital. Today he lives in Silicon Valley and works at Nutanix, a promising cloud computing startup. Both are married, and we have two adorable grandchildren, Lucas and Ana.

I Can't Stay Retired!
My husband and I recently moved to Spring Island, South Carolina, a place of incredible natural beauty. We are making new friends and continuing with our favorite activities. I am delighted to renew my interest in horses and am enjoying riding trails canopied by live oak and Spanish moss. Only 300 families live on the Island and I miss the diversity of people who have inhabited my life. But I continue to search for opportunities to increase my knowledge of the world and to strengthen my capabilities. In the winter of 2017, I will be engaged by the Ministry of Education of the United Arab Emirates to evaluate K-12 public schools and will be spending six weeks in Abu Dhabi and Dubai. When I complete this engagement, I am certain I will continue to look for an intellectual community in which I can further expand my understanding and appreciation of our miraculous world.

Reflections
Reflecting on my career as a woman, and my professional journey since graduating from the University of Pennsylvania, I believe I have benefited from good luck and good decisions. Most importantly, I have been the beneficiary of good people. Throughout the years, I have been delighted to help many young people secure employment or school admission by calling on my large network of contacts in the various fields I have nurtured. I have never forgotten the successful individuals in my life who were generous and helpful when I needed someone to "open a door" to give me access when I had none, and to encourage me to "reach for the brass ring." I remain grateful to the men and women who gave me a chance to prove myself, who respected me for my achievements and valued my qualities.

ANNE KLEIN

A CAREER OF CORPORATE AND COMMUNITY LEADERSHIP

When students or professionals ask for advice, I say, "Never let anyone tell you can't do something. Just do it. Be willing to take a risk. Be a leader. And give back willingly."

Anne Sceia Klein

My Early Years
The choice of a college other than Penn and the Wharton School wasn't even up for discussion. I was greatly influenced by my father who told me that, as an only child, I needed to be able to support myself. "You have to go to a college where you can use your mind and not your hands," my father said. Both he and my mother urged me to study hard. In high school, I earned all As, was class valedictorian and president of the Student Council. Most of my female Penn classmates had achieved the same success.

My father was familiar with the Wharton School. Although we lived in Hammonton, N.J. (the Blueberry Capital of the World!), my father had a dental practice in Vineland, N.J. For more than 20 years he taught post-graduate dentists at Penn. Earlier, he had taught juniors and seniors.

My mother encouraged me to attend a four-year college. She had wanted to go to Drexel University (then called Drexel Institute of Technology) and major in home economics. But she was the last of nine children, and her mother didn't want her to leave home, as all her well-educated (Cornell, Penn and Temple) siblings had done. So my mother pleased her mother and was able to commute to Peirce School (now Peirce Junior College) in Philadelphia and learned all she could about business.

In 1959 when I applied to Penn, it was very difficult to get accepted as a woman. In the fall of that year, my father took me to meet Penn's Director of Admissions. A friend of my father's had arranged this meeting. I don't remember much about the interview, except I recall an answer to one question I had: "Should I take solid geometry?" The reply: "It's a good disciplinary subject." Looking back, the interview was a cordial formality. I did not take solid geometry after all.

My high school principal was very discouraging. He told my father the best he could do was help me get into a local state teachers college. My father didn't react well. Fortunately, I was accepted by Penn.

My Education at Penn

The first two years in the Wharton School offered a predetermined course of study, so I took first level economics, statistics, accounting, business law, and management, among others. I was the only woman in my classes.

I remember vividly I wanted to study financial investment and major in corporate finance. In my sophomore year, we had to secure the permission of the department chair to be able to select our major for the final two years. But the department chair would have none of my being in his classes. My recollection is that he said, "No woman will ever graduate from Penn with a degree in corporate finance as long I am chair of the department." I was furious with him.

My second choice was marketing, and I went to see the department chair. He was more liberal in his attitude toward women in his classes and said he would take me. That's how I became a marketing major.

We could select one elective each semester outside of the Wharton School curriculum to broaden our education. I chose History of the Opera and of the Symphony, Religions of the World, Shakespeare, English Literature and Philosophy. I loved those classes.

There was one optional public relations class taught by a female professional who had worked for a large agency. I will never forget Gemma Newman; she was an expert on artist Mary Cassatt and able to offer real world experience, but I don't recall her ever mentioning the challenges women would face in the business world. She appeared fearless; I took my cue from her.

Other professors with real world experience were Dr. William Kelley in advertising and Charles Webber, Esq., in business law. Those three individuals did so much to encourage me.

Women's Issues and Networking

Many of my professors invited outside speakers to their classes, but none was a woman. The speakers were heads of ad agencies, marketing companies and marketing research firms. I don't recall having any seminars in which women in the workplace was ever discussed.

We had not discussed any dress for business success code when we were undergraduates, but we had very strong social and dress guidelines at Penn. Women couldn't wear pants to classes or outside the dorm. We couldn't go to the dining room unless we were properly dressed. The Penn guidelines were clear. I think that helped a lot in terms of being prepared for the real-world business dress code.

I don't recall any Wharton women's organization at the time. There were only 12 women in my Wharton School freshman class. We were told we were the biggest class of women ever to enter Wharton as undergraduates. There was one female full professor, Dr. Dorothy Brady, who taught economic history. I'll never forget her. She was assigned as advisor to the women, and she did the best she could to help us. But she had no power or influence.

The term "networking" also did not exist, especially among women. I don't recall being encouraged to join the Marketing Club or any other club where I might have met future business connections. After graduation, networking became the key to my success.

At job fairs, when recruiters came to campus, it was not unusual to see "Male Only" printed at the end of a job posting for marketing training programs. "Girls didn't pump gas; girls didn't stock shelves," we were told. I was so naïve; I had no clue that the "male only" designation was a not-so-subtle way of keeping women out of the workplace. I also did not realize that women who did manage to make it into the workplace were often being paid less than men who were working at the same job.

When I finished my four years at Wharton, none of the few jobs available to me appealed to me. I decided to take another route to a career and enrolled in the Annenberg School for Communication (ASC) for a master's degree in communication. My father encouraged me to go to law school, but after spending four years in classes with all men, I could not face another three years as, no doubt, the only girl in the class.

The Penn Influence
Despite the obstacles to landing a marketing job, when I left Penn I had a great deal of confidence; I felt I could conquer the world. No doubt I had received the best education available, and no one could ever challenge my education or credentials. Perhaps I was more confident than I should have been, but with encouragement from my parents, plus my Penn education, I plowed ahead. Nothing intimidated me.

Being a female student at Wharton did have some advantages. It taught me how to be a "team player" and get along with the men in my classes.

They liked me, and they helped me. This was the basis for developing my leadership style which has been collaborative and cooperative.

When I graduated, I was clueless about what to expect in the "man's world" out there. If I found myself hitting a concrete wall, or wanting to earn more money, or saw an opportunity that looked good, I just took the chance and applied for the next job. Some moves worked out; others did not.

There was no direct career path for me. I took advantage of whatever opportunities presented themselves. Penn definitely gave me the confidence to just "go for it."

The Beginning of My Career—and the 50-Year Journey
After graduating from Annenberg, I made up my mind to take the first job offered in marketing. Meanwhile, I also decided to take a class in speedwriting. I'd start as a secretary if I had to. That is how most women broke into the marketing world back in the mid-60s.

I contacted placement services, but most only worked with men. I didn't give up. I contacted the head of Penn's "Women's Placement Service" (which was separate from the regular [i.e. men only] Placement Service). She was accustomed to placing nurses and teachers. She knew only one woman in business, who was an assistant editor of an insurance company magazine. I connected with that woman who knew another woman recruiter who had just placed a woman as a public relations director. This one connection began my career. I went to work for that PR director and had my start.

I had to deal with some less than understanding treatment by men in business, but it was subtle, and even concealed. At my first job, I made $75.00 a week. Based on my Annenberg classmates' salaries at $50.00 a week, I guess I didn't do too bad. When I was working at my first news briefing, one of the reporters filed a story with this as the lead: "There was a pretty blonde hostess who presided over a coffee urn and a pile of press kits." That was awful. I don't think the reporter realized how much he demeaned me. But at the time, educated working women in marketing were seen only as hostesses or secretaries. Being young, I was perceived by men in the business world as just a "cute kid," not a well-educated woman. My "little Mary Sunshine" attitude probably didn't help.

I stayed in my first job for five months and then was offered a PR Director position at the Pennsylvania state Christmas Seal organization. I went from $75 a week to $115 a week, a big jump in salary in those days. The executive director I worked for was very professional. The senior vice president was a woman, and an executive vice president was a gentleman who also was very supportive. It was a great experience.

After winning a national public relations award for the best PR program among Christmas Seal organizations, I was pirated by a PR consultant and went to an architectural firm, where I faced a totally different culture. That job lasted only a year, because my boss did not support me. Even his secretary would not help me. She said, "I don't work for little girls."

Meanwhile, I had become involved in professional organizations and met a man who became my mentor. Through his contacts, he learned there was a position opening up at Girard Bank (now Citizens Bank). I was interviewed by the senior vice president of marketing, and we got along fabulously from the start. I

I had the privilege of presenting to President Ford a petition, signed by a million Philadelphians, asking for the original Declaration of Philadelphia to be returned to Philadelphia for the observance of the U.S. Bicentennial in 1976. Ford sent the Stone Plate, the original copper engraving from which facsimile copies were printed.

knew there would be a middle person — a VP of advertising and marketing — so I waited 6 months for him to be hired. I interviewed and got the job; I was there for seven years. I loved every minute, did well, and was promoted to a second level officer in 4 years — unheard of in the world of bank promotions at the time.

I was involved in many very public activities at Girard Bank, like putting the first bike racks in Center City Philadelphia. We published books with our annual reports, and I hosted lunch for the authors, such notables as author James Michener, architect Louis Kahn, and chairman of the New York Stock Exchange James Needham. We accompanied the All-Philadelphia Boys Choir to the former Soviet Embassy in Washington, D.C. and accompanied the Philadelphia Flyers and the Stanley Cup to children's hospitals and senior homes.

Thinking I needed to get back into finance, I left Girard Bank and made the biggest mistake of my career. My "director of financial communications" job lasted just three months. The man I was working for spent his day on personal business; then at 5 pm each evening, he began working on company business. I would arrive home at midnight every night. I resigned the day I returned from my honeymoon. The vice president of the company asked what I wanted? I knew I could not sue the company; I'd never get another job. So I said, "I'm not going to sue you, but I've got a file an inch thick detailing the abuse I've taken. If you can say my job was eliminated, I will walk away." I had just married; we had a mortgage. The unemployment check would pay our mortgage.

Spending 7 months unemployed should have been enjoyable. I regret I did not enjoy it, as I worried about getting back to work. And I still faced instances of discrimination. At one interview with INA, the Vice President of Public Relations sat back in his chair with his feet on the desk. As I looked at the soles of his shoes, he asked me when I planned to get pregnant. I later told the man who had recommended me. He said, "You can sue, but you'll never get another job."

Finally, a friend who headed a PR firm persuaded one of his friends to hire me at his agency, but at the same salary I had been paid at the bank, not the higher one I had after that. Another issue was my new boss had no idea of what to do with a woman who had never done PR for cosmetics or consumer products. Fortunately, I was assigned to work with the research department of a brokerage firm. That assignment was a big success. But a comment I will never forget is (as I was told by my boss) that the CFO of another client corporation said he "could not work with someone who reminded him of a contemporary of his daughter."

After about a year, I applied for and was named Manager of Media Relations at the headquarters of Sun Co. (Sunoco). I had a great deal of responsibility leading the corporate media relations department of seven staff members and assisting the many PR people in the subsidiaries.

Twenty-four hours before I joined Sun, one of its refineries had over-pressurized and overfilled an underground butane cavern. Through a sequence of events, nine houses had their heating units catch fire. Thankfully, no one was killed. Having to deal with this situation on my first day of a new job was truly a baptism by fire!

Six months later, our company announced it had to start allocating heating oil and then the Iranian hostage crisis caused another gasoline shortage. This was the beginning of my extensive experience in crisis and issues communication. Working for an oil company, I had to deal with numerous incidents and issues on a daily basis and became really good at

Aboard a gas platform as part of a familiarization tour of Sun Oil facilities in the Gulf of Mexico.

managing these scenarios. As a result of my work with the staff and the media, I was promoted to Manager of Executive Communication, working with only the top 13 officers of the company. My job was to keep them visible to the media and the public.

I was never able to reach the executive compensation level at Sun, although I was very close — within a relatively few ranking points below the threshold. I had worked hard, only to reach a dead end, with no professional ladder to climb. I was discouraged and considered leaving the company. Once again, my father helped me. We discussed the option of starting my own business. He asked me, "What do you have to lose?" My husband Jerry was practicing law by that time, and I responded, "Nothing."

Taking the Entrepreneurial Plunge — Anne Klein Communications Group, LLC

I started Anne Klein Communications Group (AKCG), a public relations consulting firm, with one client in 1982 — Sun Company — and retired on January 3, 2017, the firm's 35th anniversary. AKCG now employs 10 people and 4 senior counselors and focuses on crisis and issues communication, along with media relations and spokesperson training. Because of my background, the firm also became known for community outreach and environmental communications.

In mid-2004, I had hired a young man just out of college who showed tremendous professional promise. It was the best hire of my career. After 10-years of transition, he now is the president and sole owner and continues the firm's specialties in my footsteps.

Me, our firm's new president Chris Lukach, and husband Jerry (far right) receiving a congratulatory joint resolution of the New Jersey Legislature from State Senator Dawn Addiego on the occasion of our firm's 35th anniversary.

The Personal Side

When I graduated from college, I was independent, outspoken and driven. Not too much changed, but then everything changed. I met Jerry Klein when I was working at Girard Bank; he was an assistant editor at a local business magazine. Our bank was the first in the area to sell gold, and Jerry was assigned to write that story. He also was working as a reporter (and later editor and news anchor) at Philadelphia's all-news radio station, KYW.

We married in 1976, and Jerry decided to attend law school. He graduated in 1980 and spent five years with a large Philadelphia law firm as a litgator. Two years later, I began AKCG. Jerry would work all day at the law firm, then come home in the evening to edit copy for me and assist with agreement letters and financial matters. After 3½ years of trying to manage a law career and helping me, he joined AKCG fulltime.

As an only child, I had to look after my parents in their later years as their health declined. I hired caregivers. Sometimes we had more staff at my parents' home than we had working in our PR firm. Jerry helped tremendously by taking on some of my professional activities. For example, he took my place as treasurer of Pinnacle Worldwide, an international network of public relations firms. With commitment and hard work, Jerry eventually became president, chairman and chairman emeritus. Both of us have traveled worldwide and have given speeches as far away as Singapore, Australia and New Zealand.

Although both of us are technically "retired," Jerry has a contract to continue working with the CFO, maintaining the computer system and managing the office administration. I am marketing and introducing our president to new contacts I meet.

Several of my classmates mentioned the benefit of having a supportive spouse. It has been a great journey working with Jerry for more than three decades.

Giving Back to Students and the Community
While I recall giving speeches to communications professionals, I can't recall speaking to any students at Penn until I had my own business. I went back and spoke only once at Wharton and several times at Annenberg. Evidently what I had to say was different from anything ASC was teaching. After one of the lectures — probably in 1988 or 1989 — a group of students called me and asked if they could come to our office. They asked me, "Would you please teach us what a press kit is, and what a biographical sketch is, and what a news release looks like?" We arranged a time, met and the students were happy.

Over the years, I did not keep up enough with Wharton as I probably should have, but I was more involved in being on boards of nonprofit organizations like the Philadelphia Citizens Council for Clean Air and Pennsylvania Pro Musica, a baroque music group. I also actively volunteered for the Girl Scouts and was deeply involved with the Philadelphia chapter of the Public Relations Society of America (PRSA). First I chaired PRSA committees, then moved up the officer ranks and later became president of the Philadelphia chapter, finally chairing the Mid-Atlantic District and serving 12 years as assembly delegate to the PRSA national organization. I also served on the Executive Committee of the PRSA Counselors Academy.

In 2004, I was inducted into the Philadelphia Public Relations Association Hall of Fame. More recently, I became chair of the Central/Southern New Jersey Board of the American Heart Association, and worked on the Go Red for Women movement for 10 years, seeking personal donations.

For nearly 35 years I have been a member of Philadelphia's Forum of Executive Women, and I still serve on the advisory board of *SJ Magazine*.

I frequently spoke to students throughout the Philadelphia region and, for 32 years, I served as professional advisor to communications students at Rowan University (Glassboro, N.J.) and never said "no" to a student who wanted advice. For these years of service, I received a national award as Outstanding Professional Advisor and was inducted into the Rowan University PR Hall of Fame.

Personal Reflections

I did whatever I had to do to keep my career going. I concentrated on networking and giving back. Networking was the key to my success; I became the ultimate "connector." People remember what you did for them. All I ever asked in return was to make sure AKCG made their short list when the time came they needed PR services.

Two management consultants observed that I never learned to say "no." That's very true. I helped everyone who asked, and my willingness to help grew my business.

I'm proud of the recognition our firm has received over the years. We have won dozens of awards as judged by our peers. I was recognized as a Woman of Distinction by *Philadelphia Business Journal*, named as one of the top 50 women in business by *NJ Biz* in the second year of their program, selected as a Brava Award winner by *Smart CEO Magazine*, and in 2017 was honored with a Lifetime Achievement Award from the Philadelphia chapter of the Public Relations Society of America.

Speaking at the Rowan University graduate commencement ceremony in 2012.

FAYE C. LAING, M.D.

AN INTERNATIONAL PIONEER
IN DIAGNOSTIC ULTRASOUND

Throughout my life, I have considered myself fortunate to have been in the right place at the right time. In May 2017, I was privileged to receive a prestigious "Women Making History Award" from the National Women's History Museum. Currently this museum has an online presence, but the expectation is high that a physical structure will soon be built on the Washington, D.C. mall to commemorate women who have made an impact on our country. I feel honored to have been chosen to receive this award, but realize the path leading to this accolade was a curved one, with many intervening branches and potential stumbling blocks. Without doubt, my undergraduate experience at the University of Pennsylvania was formative, and played a pivotal role in helping me traverse this path and in establishing who I am today.

Faye C. Natanblut Laing, M.D.

My Early Years

My childhood had some truly shaky moments, including a prolonged hospitalization that left me so weak I could not attend kindergarten with my friends. When I began the first grade, I was placed in the class for slow learners. Fortunately, my father, Milton Natanblut, who emigrated as a teenager from Poland, did not agree with the school's assessment. Although he had only three years of formal education, he strongly believed once you could read, you could do anything. On most evenings, therefore, we spent time reading together. I don't recall having access to typical children's books; newspaper editorials were more his style. Upon reflection, I now realize how pivotal his guidance and support were. Once I could read, I quickly caught up to my peers and had no further problems learning the "three R's."

I grew up in Bay Ridge section of Brooklyn, N.Y., primarily a 'blue collar' neighborhood, and attended a public high school (Fort Hamilton), which did not emphasize academic or career guidance. There were some honors classes, however, and I was fortunate to be included with these students. For as long as I can remember, and no doubt influenced by my childhood illness, I wanted to be a nurse. My parents, however, kept trying to steer my career aspirations toward teaching. Being a middle child, however, I was convinced I knew better, and nursing remained at the top of my list.

My plan was to go directly from high school into a three-year nursing school program. Fortunately, several events converged that led me to take a different path. First, as a third-year high school student, I was approached by several teachers who encouraged me to consider college. Also, the following summer, as a junior camp counselor, I was exposed to several senior counselors who were attending college and lived away from home; this sounded very appealing. Finally, my older brother was attending a tuition-free college, so the money my father had carefully accumulated for his education might be steered in my direction. I now had a new plan, which was to attend a four-year college and obtain both my R.N. and B.S. degrees. My parents also agreed with my desire to leave "the nest," provided I live not more than 100 miles from home.

My Penn Experience
In the fall of 1960, my new life began at the University of Pennsylvania. To my way of thinking, attending an out-of-town college provided an important exodus from my provincial and protected environment; indeed, I was emerging from a cocoon. As a college freshman, my nursing courses were all introductory in nature. My other courses and additional outside activities provided a smorgasbord that I relished sampling. Again, a series of "happenings" ultimately led me toward a different pathway. I started to date a medical student; he wanted to know if, in lieu of nursing, would I consider studying medicine? Also, a very good friend (Judith Tholfsen Brook), who was a junior at Penn, disclosed she was planning to attend Columbia University's medical school, the College of Physicians and Surgeons.

And most important and pivotal was my summer school microbiology teacher, Dr. Sidney Rodenberg, who took me aside and asked me to consider a career in medicine. I told him that given my family and upbringing, this would be impossible. He persisted and ultimately met and spoke to my parents. Although I was never privy to details of this conversation, I consider this conversation to be a life-changing event. As a result, on my first day as a sophomore, I went to Penn's administrative office, withdrew from Nursing School and with no questions asked, was permitted to matriculate into the College for Women. In those days, women in medicine were few and far between, and given I was reasonably insecure, I could not commit to a pre-med curriculum. After sampling a wide variety of courses, I eventually majored in Art History and minored in Biology. I soon discovered, however, that my microbiology teacher, Dr. Rodenberg, also was a Premedical Advisor, and with his continued encouragement, support and guidance, I decided to study medicine.

Thanks to a very strong letter of support from Dr. Rodenberg, and following in the footsteps of my friend Judith Tholfsen Brook, I began a new chapter of my life in the fall of 1964, matriculating at Columbia University's College of Physicians and Surgeons (P & S). As an interesting aside, during my medical school interview with the Dean, I made it clear I required financial support for this expensive education. I remember being told that women did not qualify for loans, since it would be unfair for them to enter marriage with financial debt. As a result, women were given scholarships.

My Medical Career Begins
P & S was one of the most liberal schools with respect to allowing women to study medicine, and women accounted for almost 10% of our class (we were 12 of 125 students). Even more interesting is we gained two additional women, and our graduating class consisted of 99 individuals with 14 women. In comparison, Penn's Medical School was more typical, with approximately 4% women. I found the first two years of medical school relatively boring, as there was so much memorization. Beginning in my third year, however, when I was finally exposed to caring for patients, I became committed, and realized that medicine and I were meant for one other.

My Columbia Med School graduation photo

Eventually, I encountered another challenge, which was to choose an area of specialization. Following medical school graduation, and after spending two years in internal medicine at Columbia Presbyterian Medical Center, another convergence occurred that led me toward Diagnostic Radiology. Daily interaction with the hospital radiologists made me realize the pivotal role the radiologists played in helping determine what afflicted many of my patients. The radiologists were medical "detectives" and this intrigued me. In particular, four radiology residents took me under their wings and mentored me. Little did we know at the time, three of these physicians ultimately would become department chairmen at prestigious medical centers (choose your mentors wisely).

New York was a dangerous place in the late 1960s, and I was held up four times; understandably, I needed to get away. The Chairman of Radiology at Presbyterian Hospital phoned his very good friend, the Chairman of Radiology at the University of California, San Francisco (UCSF), Dr. Alexander Margulis. It turned out one of the radiology residents had just been drafted and sent to Vietnam. I got the vacant position.

The Move to San Francisco – Becoming an Ultrasound Expert
My next three years were spent as a UCSF resident, training to become a radiologist. Despite the fact I was the only female, I felt accepted and was treated extremely well. I was selected as Chief Resident and subsequently was offered a faculty position at San Francisco General Hospital (SFGH), an affiliated training hospital for UCSF, recognized as an outstanding acute care and trauma facility.

At this point in my career, I envisioned becoming an angiographer, but to my dismay, my mentor left on July 1, 1973 – the very day I joined the faculty. I was asked, instead, to learn something about a new technology called "diagnostic ultrasound." The machine had just arrived; no one had experience or interest in those "funny looking"

At SFGH (middle row, left)

pictures. There I was, the new "Chief of Ultrasound," with an unwieldy dinosaur-looking piece of equipment that was actually placed in my office. With time and a lot of practice, I learned to use and even enjoy this machine – perhaps because I was entirely self-taught.

Mentors were non-existent with respect to this new form of imaging. My peers were great, and we soon formed a team of "pioneers" who began to push forward the frontiers of diagnostic ultrasound. We truly were on our own, as this was the only non-invasive cross sectional imaging modality; computed tomography (CT) and magnetic resonance imaging (MRI) were not yet available. Working in a major trauma and acute care facility for 17 years provided a plethora of interesting and challenging patients. In the 1980's, as my academic career advanced, I imaged and published the appearances of many of the "itis's" (i.e., acute cholecystitis, appendicitis, pancreatitis, etc). Patients with acute gynecological conditions, including ectopic pregnancy and pelvic inflammatory disease, were also not in short supply. Soon, a new and even more challenging group of patients came to my attention, and HIV/AIDS became new words in my vocabulary.

My experience at SFGH provided me with many opportunities. I learned how to run and administer a busy and clinically relevant service. Teaching also was a very fulfilling and rewarding part of my daily

existence. I loved using and having many opportunities to test new equipment. I especially appreciated the introduction of real-time imaging, and the challenges of understanding Doppler applications. In those days, the  ultrasound community (both professional and commercial) was relatively small, and gatherings at annual meetings was like a "family get-together."

A Move Back East to Boston and then Georgetown

By 1990, my SFGH colleagues had left and I ultimately found myself heading east to Boston to work at one of Harvard's major medical facilities, the Brigham and Women's Hospital (BWH). This provided a great opportunity to hone my obstetric ultrasound skills and to continue my interest in gynecology. One of my greatest enjoyments during this time was to work very closely with the residents in my capacity as Director of Education and Training.

Ultimately, following an almost crippling ski injury (being hit by a chair lift) in 2009, I planned to retire — and by sheer happenstance, I ended up relocating to a lovely community in the Georgetown section of Washington, D.C. There, to my great surprise, I discovered both the Chairman (James Spies, M.D.) and Vice Chairman (Cirrelda Cooper, M.D.) of the Georgetown University Hospital (GUH) Department of Radiology were my former SFGH residents. One thing led to another and for the next six years, I was thrilled to work part-time at GUH. The challenges of this ultrasound section were completely different from my prior experiences, and I became proficient at using ultrasound in conjunction with interventional procedures, as well as to evaluate a myriad of liver, kidney, and even pancreatic transplants.

Retired and Still Teaching

Now that I have been retired for two years, I thoroughly enjoy the community where I live. I take advantage of the opportunity to audit classes at Georgetown University and go to the gym on a regular basis. I would be remiss if I did not also mention I continue to see the Georgetown radiology residents on a regular basis, because I cannot resist teaching them via lectures and conferences.

As I reflect upon my 42-year career and consider the academic road I have taken, I am enormously grateful to the many individuals who have crossed my path, and who have made my career possible. I now realize my interest in imaging probably began at the University of Pennsylvania where I was drawn to art history. Critically analyzing a painting is not so different from evaluating medical images. Even though I didn't always realize it at the time, I was fortunate to have had so many incredible mentors, and to work with a team of individuals who not only were very smart, but also were team players and nice people. Admittedly, I was not often consciously aware of being "different," especially early in my career when I was frequently the only female physician. I am grateful my hard work and

Being inducted as an Honorary Fellow, Australasian College of Radiology, 1984.

dedication have been recognized. As an academic, I achieved Professor status at UCSF, Harvard and Georgetown Universities, and as a teacher, I have been the recipient of several major teaching awards. I guess I fulfilled my parents' wish for me to become a teacher.

Academic medicine satisfied a personal need, which was to live and to travel, not only throughout this country but also throughout the world. As a seasoned educator, I have set foot on every continent and have lectured in each (with the exception of Antarctica — because the penguins did not appear interested).

Most important is that my wonderful career enabled me to work with and to train thousands of young physicians and ultrasound technicians.

In my opinion, sharing what I know and providing mentorship is one of the reasons I was chosen to receive the "Women Making History" award from the National Women's History Museum.

Advice to Young Women

What advice I would give to women who express an interest in pursuing medicine? Mentors play a very important role in one's life and career. Choose them wisely.

Try to expose yourself to opportunities to be around influential and accomplished people, and don't be afraid to seize new and different opportunities.

When I first began college, I was very timid and lacked confidence. But I was fortunate to meet individuals who believed in me and who counseled me. This eventually provided me with a deep belief in myself, which in turn allowed me to move forward and succeed.

Don't be afraid when faced with unforeseen opportunities, and seek out new challenges. Since you never know what's around the next corner, it's worth exploring and what you discover may just change your life forever.

Lecturing in Hong Kong, 1987.

ILENE LEFF

A SUCCESSFUL CAREER IN PRIVATE, PUBLIC AND SOCIAL SECTORS AND CONSULTING

The young people today don't know about what we did in the Sixties; they know the Sheryl Sandberg story. I hope this book opens young women's minds to what the world was like for the pioneers like the Penn Women of the Class of 1964.

Women like us have to "teach." This whole phenomenon of women rising in business over nearly 60 years has taken place with its own energy. There hasn't been a constitutional amendment. This all has come about of its own, from within. Those of us who were pioneers in the business world are surprised there is so little progress. Just recently, I saw an article from Slate magazine with the title, "Men Still Aren't Comfortable with Ambitious Women."

Ilene Leff

My Early Years

Like so many other mothers in our era, mine did not want me to go to college too far away from home. I wanted to go to an Ivy League or a Seven Sisters college. Given the constraints, there were two choices, Penn and Barnard (affiliated with Columbia University). Although I was accepted at both universities, there were no dorm rooms at Barnard, so I went to Penn. My mother was pleased because she wanted me to meet a nice guy and get married. With the Penn graduate schools of law and medicine, my mom felt if I met and married one of those students, I would have an easier life than she had as one of the first women pharmacy owners.

I went to a public high school in Union, New Jersey. Although my guidance counselor was friendly with the people at Pembroke (the women's college associated with Brown University in Rhode Island) and my best friend went to college there, I felt the weather was too cold. With the encouragement of my father — the first of his immediate family born in the U.S.A. — I studied and got all As in high school. I was ranked #1 of my class of 639 students. I was the first person in my immediate family to go away to college. Like most girls with male siblings in the 1960s, my brother received eight years of paid education, a junior year abroad and travel. I received the four years at Penn, but I paid for my own graduate school and my trip to Europe!

My Penn Experience

The *New York Times* was my reference for my major course of study at Penn. I read the want ads regularly and saw economics and statistics majors were in demand. My class schedule was allocated 50 percent to the "in demand" subjects that could "sell," and 50 percent to liberal arts. I graduated as a sociology major after majoring in math, economics and psychology.

President Kennedy was elected early in my Penn days. His famous inaugural speech quote, "Ask not what your country can do for you; ask what you can do for your country," had a huge impact on me. I have always viewed what I do as my calling to use my skills, strengths and education to make the world a better place for people.

My father was a doctor, my mother a pharmacist. My parents always told me I should help those in need. I felt privileged to be at Penn.

My first love was fashion design, but when Sputnik happened and I discovered my IQ, I changed my interest to math. Penn gave me a broad view of the world; we had knowledge and understanding of the problems in the world. I got an education in how to learn and how to solve problems. Another influence on me was The Wharton School and the guys I knew on campus who were in Wharton. The Wharton environment pervaded the campus; I took courses in Wharton.

Among my Wharton professors, Dr. Irving Kravis was my advisor and economics professor; he was very encouraging and supportive. He encouraged me to go to graduate school. When it occurred to me that people did not act rationally as economic formulas predicted, I changed my major to psychology. Another professor, Dr. Stanley Schor, taught me statistics (I will never forget going into a room filled with a computer!).

My father's expectations were always in the back of my mind, so I asked of every professor what I could do to get an A. Fortunately, we also had several female professors — in calculus, in ethics, and in folklore. They were well-known women who became role models for me because, at one point, I thought I might like to teach in college. I also recall the Dean of the College for Women, Jean Brownlee, as a role model. Dr. Margaret Mead and Ayn Rand spoke on the campus. I was encouraged by their achievements.

Another benefit of going to Penn and being in the College for Women was that we had our own extracurricular activities. This gave me the opportunity to be president of one of the houses of the women's residence hall. In addition, I was the women's fraternities and sports editor of the yearbook, a coed activity. There were many opportunities for leadership on the non-academic side. In addition, I competed with men in class. I was named the Outstanding Sophomore Woman because of my 3.8 average, leadership and service as a student tutor.

Thinking back on my college years, I realize I led two lives. During the week, I was focused on my academic studies and intellectually stimulating activities such as visiting lecturers. On the weekends, football games and fraternity parties rounded out my social side.

My Career Begins

My mother's influence continued after college graduation. I took a job as an employment counselor in New Jersey, because my mother wanted me to live at home and then get married. I did this for about a year, but felt it was too limiting and I quit my job. A trip to Europe with my good friend and classmate, Neen Hunt, broadened my views, although when I came back I did become a teacher. I dated Richard, the doctor, and Stuart, the lawyer. Marriage to either of them was the outcome my mother wanted, but I didn't marry either one because they bored me. I moved to New York in 1969, and that's when my career really started.

My Management Consulting Career

My first job was at McKinsey & Co. I had seen a want ad in *The New York Times* and it said, "college graduate: economics, statistics, finance for an international management consulting firm." I applied and got the highest test scores in statistics (Professor Schor gets all the credit for that). I was assigned to the public practice group and quickly learned that at McKinsey, men were the management consultants and the women did the calculations for them...just like the women of the movie, *Hidden Figures*.

With my statistics and communications skills, I was promoted to the research consulting staff. Again, this is where the women were slotted, regardless of their outstanding education. This group of women supported client work. While most women in research did not go to client meetings, New York Mayor John Lindsay had no trouble with women at meetings. I was at a table in a meeting with him on the day women marched for equality down Fifth Ave. The Lindsay administration had the best and brightest people of our era, and they were working hard to make the world a better place.

I owe my entire career to the men in the McKinsey public practice group. They bent over backward to be my sponsors and protectors from their colleagues who opposed women in consulting roles. With their sponsorship I was promoted to the consulting staff in 1974. Once I became a consultant, I was treated with more respect.

With my knowledge of fashion and recalling the strict dress code for women at Penn, I became an "expert" on how women in business should dress. At McKinsey, my colleagues and I were interviewed by a woman's fashion magazine on dressing for success!

When McKinsey hired a woman coach, she and I agreed I had to choose my battles. Salary-wise, there was about a 10 percent difference in pay between me and a male colleague. The reasoning was related to experience (his corporate and my teaching) and education (his MBA and my MA). Since I already had been promoted to the consulting staff, I let the salary subject go.

I found the McKinsey public practice group was more liberal and open. The executive resource management group was more traditional, and they were the holders of the concrete door; they held it solidly in place. I received one very negative performance review. The man responsible for professional development was totally supportive of me and ignored the review. We were so few women — maybe 12 out of hundreds and hundreds of men.

There were no women partners at the time I was at McKinsey and for a while after. One woman who came from Harvard Business School was determined to "make it." In terms of attitude, she wanted to be a partner. She eventually made it, and she gave 100 percent of her life to the process.

Looking Back On Women in Business in the Mid-Sixties
I recall the climate for female advancement was limited when I graduated from Penn. Teacher, nurse, secretary — those were the traditional occupations for women. In 1964, the Civil Rights Act was passed, but not much changed for several years until the women of AT&T filed suit with the Equal Employment Opportunity Commission in the early 1970s over salary differentials. Those women won millions of dollars. That famous lawsuit started the changes for women in business. And they changed the world for other women. The women who brought the lawsuit sacrificed themselves, destroying their careers. They could not find work that matched their levels of education and expertise. But they changed the way women were compensated and taken seriously.

My Move to Corporate

My area of interest was executive resources, and I became head of worldwide human resources at Revlon, when it was a Fortune 200 company. Abby Rudolph, a man who was at McKinsey, had moved on to Revlon. Marvin Bower, "the father of the consulting profession," told Rudolph to hire me, since he knew I was interested in moving on. Rudolph did hire me and became my next protector. At that point, I was paid as much or more than my peers. I know because I designed compensation policies and had information about everyone's salaries.

Women still were challenged in the business world, and I did have one encounter with a man at Revlon who was accused of having porn on his computer. He said he would schedule a meeting with me after the guard left so no one would hear me scream. He was a one-off lunatic.

While I was at Revlon and thereafter, I did everything I could to help women. I started the MBA development program and hired and coached a young woman from Columbia Business School; she is still a friend today. Then, another Revlon female staff member became pregnant. We had no policies, so we made them up as we went along.

McKinsey and Revlon gave me the opportunity to work in London, Paris, Greece and Germany, and to serve as a role model in those countries that followed the U.S.A. in starting professional roles for women.

My protector at Revlon moved on to Estée Lauder; he asked me to join him there in 1988, and I stayed there until 1992. Of course, a woman founded the company and her son, a Penn grad, built it. It was filled with women in responsible positions.

My Brief Time in Government

Continuing my JFK-inspired work, I joined the Clinton Administration in 1993 and stayed there until 1995. I was Deputy Assistant Secretary for Management at the U.S. Housing and Urban Development (HUD) department under Henry Cisneros. I was responsible for a $140 million information technology budget and 1,200 employees in 80 U.S. offices. I took the training function, reinvented it as the HUD Academy and inaugurated distance learning capabilities throughout the country.

Although I had a wonderful apartment on Pennsylvania Avenue, I really disliked Washington and went to New York on the weekends.

Return to Consulting

A McKinsey friend of mine, Bill Drayton, a MacArthur Fellow, had founded Ashoka—a social sector organization that supports social entrepreneurs—in D.C. in 1980. I began working with Ashoka in 1995 and continue to today, consulting with social entrepreneurs worldwide. In 1995, when my father became ill, I moved back to New York. Yet my father still wanted me to have a "job" job and not consult independently, so in 1997 I founded the Human Resource Strategies Consulting practice at EisnerAmper, one of the nation's largest full-service advisory and accounting firms. I stayed there until 2000.

With Howie, my significant other.

Since 2000, I've had my own consulting practice with small companies and nonprofits in all sectors including arts, culture, education, women's programs and advocacy. In addition to Ashoka, my clients include such organizations as Carnegie Hall and the Metropolitan Opera. I'm working through them "to make the world a better place for people."

Some Final Thoughts

My strong disagreement with Sheryl Sandberg, author of *Lean In*, is that she demeaned women who had to "fit in" in order to survive. Gloria Steinem agreed. I find that lacking in understanding of the challenges of working in male-dominated companies in the early days. I did everything I possibly could to assist other women. Yes, we did have to "fit in." If we hadn't helped each other and fit in, Sheryl Sandberg might not have a job today. We were the first women consultants or the first women in any role that private sector people saw; we were respected...and we fit in. We fit in, were successful and blazed the trail for those who followed. Nowadays, when I meet women, especially from McKinsey, they thank me for what we did in the early days.

With friend and classmate Neen Hunt (right) traveling in India in 2015.

"Networking" was not something I did actively; yet I am probably one of the most connected people around. I do not do "self-promotion" when I meet people. I was influenced by McKinsey's dedication to serving clients — to show genuine interest in what the client is doing and how I might serve them. That's the guiding principle of how I meet people and get to know them.

At Revlon, people were not encouraged to join outside organizations and boards, but I became a board member of the Financial Women's Association (FWA), was on the board and treasurer of the New York Human Resource People and Strategy Organization and on the Executive Committee of the U.S. Department of Labor Business Research Advisory Council. When I was at Estée Lauder, where industry service was encouraged, I was treasurer and on the board of the Fashion Group International. Those professional groups, especially FWA, gave me lifelong friends and broader leadership experience.

A Final Story

There is one story I want to tell. At Ashoka, many of the entrepreneurs have overcome some severe difficulty in their lives. I was a victim of date rape (not on the Penn campus). I missed two semesters at Penn overcoming this trauma. The women who join Ashoka have amazing ideas. Nothing is going to stop them; they just go and do.

I credit Jerry Hillman, Carter Bales and Marvin Bower of McKinsey for being incredible protectors who supported me. Women need male protectors. Regrettably, many men still have not become serious supporters of women.

In 2013, I founded the Western Connecticut Leadership program for proven leaders and accomplished professionals over 50 years of age to learn about the needs of the community and to become actively engaged. People our age still have a lot of talent and time, so we are building a whole community of like-minded people for those missing their work colleagues. The Leadership program keeps people actively engaged as nonprofit board members, pro bono consultants and change makers.

Penn is a great school and, now, it may be greater than it was when we were there. But I think it was really difficult for women to get in back then. There are only 385 women in the Class of 1964 at Penn in the entire world. I have friends who got into Seven Sister schools and did not get into Penn. I continue to hear this story from my Wellesley friend who has never forgotten she was not admitted to Penn.

While we were individually in the trenches on our own, I believe we did have a movement backing us. Betty Friedan and Gloria Steinem did the "promotion" for the women's movement in the 1970s. The women of our class were the operations people.

A Bit of Advice
My advice to young women in the business world today is to evaluate sector by sector, "How open is that sector for women?" The closer you are to the money—to the financial services industry—the tougher it is for women. Women also need to look at ethics—how ethical is the industry? When you have knowledge of a specific functional area where you excel, then you can move to different industries. Whatever you like, the industry doesn't matter.

Women coming out of college today don't have to spend their time fighting the battles the Penn women of 1964 had to fight. They are smart, and they have role models. Plus, they have achieved outstanding accomplishments while they were in college.

It's OK to be ambitious. My college education at Penn gave me the credentials and the courage to succeed. And, yes, I did learn to "fit in" while helping other women...and men.

RUTH MESSERSMITH

A LIFE "SPELLED OUT" BY DECADES

In the fall of 1960, we were part of a new generation of gifted girls beginning college on the brink of massive technological and societal change. All around us the rules were changing, rules that governed our bodies and questioned our future personal roles as well as our potential as professional women. Swirling around us were changes liberalizing the culture in which we lived, and it felt almost as though we were standing still in the midst of a maelstrom. Looking back, I feel fortunate to have spent time in the company of such extraordinarily bright and capable women, for they consistently nudged me to be a better me.

In the ensuing decades, we became instrumental in bridging generations — bringing forward, reshaping, and redefining not only the collegiate experience but also initiating changes in the workplace and the world in which we live. We began college as anxious high school graduates and emerged as talented, insightful women eager to take on new experiences. None of us was the same, nor were we imitations of one another. Our lives have taken on different, curious and, most certainly, a stunning array of intriguing challenges.

Ruth Wolff Fields Messersmith

Early Educational Influences

I attended Germantown Friends School, an innovative private Philadelphia Quaker school that was ahead of its time. The school valued equal education for both men and women. Fundamental to the Quakers and the school's curriculum was, and remains, emphasis on responsible citizenship. Students participated in weekend work projects that influenced neighborhood improvement to encourage local pride. Retrospectively, no doubt it was this forceful influence that kick-started my life-long appreciation of effective volunteerism.

Such formative experiences provided a unique perspective on the world and produced impressionable students with a sense of less self and more accountability towards a greater community. The high scholastic demands instilled strong principles and enduring values, underscored by the school emblem of a toga-clad figure bursting through a doorway with the motto: "*Behold, I have set before thee an open door and no man shall close it.*" For each of us, this motto meant that persistence and hard work were unquestionably the tools of success.

Selecting Penn
When time came to select a college, I'm grateful that my parents influenced me to select Penn rather than an all-women's school.

Only one of my parents was born in this country. In 1912, at the age of fifteen, my father completed gymnasium-level studies on a full scholarship at a boarding school in Germany and emigrated to meet his family already settled in the United States. He would have been satisfied had I found true love following high school, married, and raised a large family. On the other hand, my mother regularly stated that she would *never* come to see me walk down the marital aisle before she saw me walk down the aisle to pick up a college diploma. She very much regretted completing only "Normal School" with a teaching credential although, during my collegiate years, she completed art studies at the Barnes Foundation and regularly audited courses at Temple University. Indeed, she emphasized the importance of college and graduate degrees, and prevailed upon her five children — most of whom achieved *summa* and *magna cum laude* degrees with distinction as well as graduate and professional degrees.

Both of my parents were proud when I was admitted to Penn. The University's urban and physical environment, its excellent academic reputation, and the favorable ratio of men to women (5:1, but of course) met major qualifications on *my* "bucket list." And I was not disappointed.

Living on campus for all four of my undergraduate years, away from the protective shield of caring parents and four older brothers, I grew up, developed friendships, and acquired independence. Strong support and encouragement from my sorority sisters and roommates (including classmates Judy Roth Berkowitz, Susan Oppenheim Jaffe, Bryn Roberts Cohen and Gail Frank Koppman) were essential to my survival during those years. Many of those early bonds remain strong to this day. No doubt, if I lived closer today, I'd be active in University life and Penn alumni activities.

Choosing a Major and a Career
Sociology was my major because of my interest in understanding human behavior. I minored in English Literature because of my abiding regard for writing.

Looking back, it's easy to see a pattern leaning toward a Sociology major. The summer before entering Penn, I served three months as a counselor at a camp for underprivileged, inner city youth. Later, as an undergraduate, I worked two summers as an intern for the Philadelphia Department of Public Welfare creating programs in support of challenged youth and making regular home visits to pare down caseloads of overworked social workers. No doubt, these experiences were instrumental in forming my early career goal of becoming a social worker. Another undergraduate summer was a rite of passage — traveling Europe as an exchange student in Germany.

My interest in reporting, writing about or recording human behavior was nursed along by another source. While we were undergraduates, the Annenberg School of Communication and its unique curriculum came into being. In addition to my conventional academic regimen, I enjoyed several new courses offered through Annenberg. In fact, I was actually recruited for a position in Germany by a visiting lecturer from a worldwide advertising agency with an aggressive policy for hiring women with linguistic skills. I neither pursued a career in social work nor did I consider the agency opportunity overseas. Instead, I opted for marriage to a medical student!

Penn's dynamic liberal arts curriculum of that time encouraged all students to learn new ideas without confining them to act as round pegs to round holes in academic boxes. Yes, several professors "helped" and "influenced" choices I made, but I do NOT recall any who actually became involved in my personal decisions, discussed in depth the role of women in the workplace, ever mentioned the term "entrepreneurship," invited me to or announced a job fair, discussed a "dress for business success" code, or introduced "successful women" to any class where I was in attendance. I already knew about inequities in the "primarily male-dominated workplace" and was, perhaps, just naive enough not to be intimidated by it all.

In fact, lodged in my memory is part of a speech given by Vice Dean of Women Anne B. Spears, at our Freshman Retreat, just prior to matriculation. There we were, sitting cross-legged on the floor, as she stood and advised us that college was important for each of us because our education in the next four years would enable us to remain current with — and interesting to — the men we would someday marry! That speech left a wide-eyed freshman with an unpalatable sense of disappointment in a would-be academic mentor.

Still, some 29 years later at our 25th Class Reunion in 1989, I experienced yet another memory jolt which reminded me of those early years of age-old-and-readily-accepted gender bias experiences. At the Class Picnic, a handsome man walked up to me and smirked: *"I wouldn't get away with it today, would I?"* I had no trouble recognizing him. He still sported his trademark wide smile, blue denim shirt, and elbow patches sewn on his tweed blazer. The gentleman was E. Digby Baltzell, a well-known Wharton School professor and author of *The Protestant Establishment: Aristocracy and Caste in America* (in which he coined the phrase WASP or White Anglo Saxon Protestant). Baltzell then expressed regret for the B-plus final grade he'd bestowed on me in my senior year (after I'd made monumental effort for a top grade). Back then I'm not sure how I summoned the courage to make the inquiry, but upon receiving my final grade I went to his office and asked how I could have improved my work. Some quarter-century later, neither of us had forgotten his 1964 response. Back then, he simply looked at me and said, "You wrote a perfect exam. Your whole year has been a perfect experience. We just don't give As to women in the Wharton School."

Because of courses like statistics, the "Sociology Major" was not governed under the aegis of the College for Women but rather ruled by those in the halls of Wharton. This same sorry scenario recurred for me (and probably other women Sociology students), no matter how seriously I applied myself. My grade averages may have suffered, but I learned much about perspectives and policies with regard to gender bias. Remember, I was raised by older brothers and, instead of finding myself intimidated, apparently these lessons forced me to fashion new means of presenting and applying my skills and abilities — driving home never to give up on any goal or objective.

My Journalism Career Begins

A couple of months following graduation, I married my fledgling physician and, notwithstanding the Wharton experience, became assistant editor of the University's alumni magazine, *The Pennsylvania Gazette*.

In those days, the *Gazette* was a 40-page monthly publication with a circulation of over 90,000. It enjoyed the largest circulation of any alumni publication nationwide and was prepared solely by Editor Robert M. "Dusty" Rhodes and me. Dusty taught me so much about publishing and editing, frequently "blue-penciling" my articles with the admonition that alumni read differently than English professors.

My meager University salary was barely sufficient to support the two of us (my spouse's annual salary as an intern was $1,800 — which included an extra $600 because he couldn't make use of the room and board portion of his training). And although the hours were long, I felt my *Gazette* salary was commensurate with other collegiate writing opportunities across the country.

Dusty was a patient teacher who encouraged research and gave me challenging assignments. Together, we attended national meetings of alumni editors and published journalists where he graciously introduced me to seasoned writers as his equal. During my tenure there, we never missed a deadline as we produced a monthly, multiple-year award-winning publication, including the exceptional issue celebrating the Bicentennial of Medical Education. I worked at the *Gazette* up until the birth of my first son in 1967 (at which time there was no mention of anything even similar to "maternity leave" in the workplace; it was a concept waiting to be "born").

In 1970, following the birth of our second son and at the height of the Vietnam War, the military assigned my spouse to duty at the Army hospital at Fort Ord (population: 80,000), California. We moved 3,000 miles across the country and, with time to spare from my young family, I spent the next two years playing the role of an officer's wife (reorganizing the post's Medical Wives group and initiating programs which provided extra funding and food for families of enlisted and non-commissioned officers who subsisted on low incomes while their spouses were serving overseas).

Changing Tracks

My interest in returning to work or graduate school was delayed again in 1972 when our family's next move took us to Sacramento, California, where my spouse entered private medical practice. At that time, without my input, my spouse decided that I should remain at home full-time with our children. Regrettably, he was convinced that were I to return to paid employment, it would reflect poorly on his ability to financially support his family and have a negative impact on our new community's view of him.

And I went along with the idea. I drove carpools, taxied to ballgames, baked, bartered, and barbequed. I served on the Sacramento Museum and History Commission, became active in the Junior League, was President of the Country Day School Parents' Association and sat as well as a school trustee. I served on numerous community coalitions, and as an executive on the Sacramento Medical Auxiliary Board.

Still, I just longed for more. My education was static, I was frustrated with stamina to burn which jogging around my neighborhood couldn't quell, and I struggled privately to organize my energies into full-time community volunteerism. I studied our city's non-profit organizations from the American Cancer Society (ACS) to local non-profits which relied heavily on the benevolence of Sacramento donors. And my volunteer career became more consuming than full-time paid employment.

I raised money, wrote community block grants, gave tours through the historical district known as Old Sacramento, wrote the tour guide for the Junior League docents and targeted provision of educational health information to children of under-served populations for the Sacramento Medical Auxiliary.

For ACS and other organizations I wrote newsletters, outlined grant proposals and funding propositions, served on volunteer action committees, and headed civic projects. I "worked for" the Sacramento Symphony League and the city's Opera Guild; participated in bringing the Susan G. Komen Breast Cancer Foundation to Sacramento; was a founding member of a now-national group known as People Reaching Out (which emphasizes education and early intervention of teenage and childhood alcohol and substance abusers); and, for nearly 40 years, provided support for and to the Sacramento Childrens' Home (either as a member of a governing board or a committee chair) and its newer offshoot, the Sacramento Crisis Nurseries, for which I served as a board member and then president.

Most important, I learned to build collaborative efforts across groups and organizations which focused on the health and well-being of young children. Significant attention was focused on at-risk infants and children from birth through the age of five years in an effort to help families achieve stability.

Frankly, I didn't spend any time thinking about the hours and days expended, I just did it. And, while I was busy, I was more than satisfied.

Re-entering the Workforce
After eighteen years of marriage, during which I successfully raised two sons and completed decades of unpaid roles in productive leadership with those public and private non-profit organizations, I became a cliché—what's better known as a "divorcee in search of a job." Initially, I was eager and more than a little ready to rejoin the salaried work force. But the excitement was dulled when I found that potential employers did not value the knowledge and skills I'd acquired in the years spent as a committed volunteer leader. In short, I was advised that my University of Pennsylvania degree was outdated and that in order to become eligible for a "reeeal job," I was obliged to complete another academic degree. So, once again, off I went.

Despite pressure to attend law school or study real estate, I decided otherwise. In the early 1980s, the State of California was enjoying a successful economic run and high employment. It was the site of multiple military bases with allied engineering opportunities. It was experiencing growth not only in the construction industry but also in diversifying governmental agencies. California had become home to major international corporations as well as world-recognized educational institutions, and was going through rapid growth in urban areas as it was developing multiple college and junior college campuses to meet the needs of an increasing population.

Realizing this, I chose to focus on government, education, and the workings of federal, state, and local government systems. My target became a Masters in Public Administration (MPA) and a special graduate credential in Intergovernmental Management with emphasis on systems management (federal, state and local government systems and how they respond to community needs). I became part of a multi-campus graduate program of the University of Southern California (USC) with a curriculum that demanded I find a job that lasted at least through a semester's concentration relative to each area of study — local, state, and federal government. As a single mother with two sons still in school locally, I petitioned and was permitted to complete the state and local portions of my graduate studies in Sacramento at the USC Capital Campus. The federal portion followed about two years later in Washington, D.C.

The first internship was with the California Manufactures Association where I worked under two of the very best: Robert T. Monagan, former Speaker of the California State Assembly and later president of the California Economic Development Corporation; and John K. Geoghegan, later State Secretary of Business, Transportation and Housing. Those two gentlemen walked me through the halls of state government, explained differences in representation at the city and state levels, and introduced me to the stratagems of policy-making.

For direct State experience, I took a position with the State Senate Office of Research, a nonpartisan policy office that provides research for Senate members and committees for the development of effective public policy. In that role I was challenged by Office Director Elisabeth Kersten to investigate and report on a relatively new State concern, pesticides — their usage and the health effects of human exposure to these substances. This concern was to motivate and control the focus of my studies and body of work for several years.

To that date, written material was predominantly expressed in rigorous scientific journals, and I had no such background on which to call. For my investigation I used the Capital's extensive resources to conduct an international library search on all pesticides being used in specific geographical areas. To provide creditability to my report, I solicited experts at the University of California Davis to interpret the studies in exchange for recognition for their assistance. Once all the information was clarified, I was able to use their findings to produce a final report for the State Senate entitled, *The Health Effects of Human Exposure to Pesticides: Carcinogenic, Mutagenic and Teratogenic.*

In 1985, my financial security made it critical that I find that "reeeal job." And I felt pressure to complete the federal segment of my degree in order to finalize the MPA. Setting up the move to Washington, D.C. took some planning as my sons were adolescents, still living at home and heavily into high school football. I had no interest in uprooting them for a temporary situation and so arrangements were made with both their father and a live-in nanny. Additional help was volunteered by a former sorority sister and roommate, J. Patricia Sarlin Klewans (who lived outside of Washington). Patty graciously offered her assistance in meeting me at the airport and getting me settled. In the end, I packed five suitcases and quickly moved 3,000 miles. The Friday I deplaned in Washington, I didn't know where I was going to live or work, only that I had to report to USC's Capitol Center and began classes the following week.

Initially, I lucked into an interview at the Pentagon where I was handed what was then called a Government Form 171 (a one-page, two-sided piece of paper on which I was to write everything I'd done previously in the workplace). My interviewer said, "Okay, you haven't worked in 20 years. If it's all volunteer stuff, write down everything you've done in those years, including the number of people you managed for each activity, what was achieved, how many people you influenced, how much money was raised, what you learned and what skills were needed to get to the bottom line." Fortunately, he also assigned two women to help me complete the form. My 171 Form ran 17 pages.

Shortly thereafter, I was fortunate to land a serious, more relevant internship in the California Governor's Washington office as a result of my previous State research work. The pesticide issue was looming as a state and federal conundrum. Birds from Mexico to Canada were touching down in California's reservoirs during their migratory periods. In so doing, they were being critically affected by runoff waters from agricultural lands which were heavily contaminated by sickening pesticides. So, not only were Californians (especially migrant workers) and their livestock at risk, but the risk innate in certain pesticides was becoming an international issue both north and south of our border.

I chose not to remain in Washington for more than my educational needs, but preferred to return home to my children. Appreciative personnel in the California Governor's Washington office recommended me for a position in a new State health division that was being formed, and I accepted. However, no sooner did I return to Sacramento in 1988 than the new agency and its promised position were written out of a quickly declining budget.

The next two years included lots of travel, a startup public relations firm of my own, a brief diversion stint at modeling, and some freelance writing. Then, in 1990, I enthusiastically accepted the opportunity to work as Special Assistant to the new Chancellor of the California State University system with responsibility to help write his public presentations as well as to set up fund development programs on the then 19 campuses throughout the state. Once again, I was fortunate to find myself working for a bright and highly successful gentleman, Dr. Barry Munitz, who appreciated and promoted the capabilities of women.

Working for Dr. Munitz, I traveled constantly throughout the State explaining the need to increase tuitions to unhappy college presidents and urging the

During my brief modeling career.

development of funding sources for each campus. For nearly a year, I lived out of a hotel in Long Beach and a series of suitcases on the road. I became numb to anything not work-related, and utterly exhausted. It took another year for me to realize that this was my "concrete wall," a personal setback if you will, and one pretty much of my own making. It was, once again, time to return to Sacramento to seek a position closer to family and home.

Re-entering Life

In December of 1993, following lunch with two colleagues whose help I had enlisted on my search for a new job, I was sent to interview with a man whose company not only managed a large number of non-profit associations but also provided an executive search service for companies and agencies. What started as an interview and a not-so-blind date became a friendship that turned into romance and later into a wonderful marriage.

Dr. Lloyd E. Messersmith and I were married in December of 1994. Together we have three sons, three daughters-in-law, and five wonderful grandchildren — each living locally.

Lloyd and me in Cabo in 2013.

With my posse, the grandkids.

Over these past 23 years, Lloyd has generously given me the gifts of contentment and encouragement. He is my unflappable sounding board and editor, as well as an even-tempered and persevering partner. He has vigorously supported my return to committed volunteerism, and motivated me to develop critical programs and projects that touch the lives of abused and neglected children in our community. And, in 2001, Lloyd joined me for a special trip to Ireland, where he cheered me on to complete the Dublin marathon in order to raise funds to fight childhood arthritis.

Even in "retirement," I've continued to take on Board positions, provide mentoring to non-profit groups, and remain active in programs that encourage continuing education. In 2011, the Junior League of Sacramento presented me with their Community Star Award in front of several hundred community colleagues.

Since then I've served on the Executive Board of the University of California Davis Medical/Health Center's Community Advisory Board, and as a founding member of the Cabinet for the Betty Irene Moore School of Nursing at UC Davis. And though I've recently decided to step back from such a frenetic pace, I'm still involved with a local "Stop Falls" coalition and a program of community courses that educate citizens over

55 on how to improve mobility and awareness of potential health and fall hazards, and to maintain better balance in their lives.

Passing Along Some Lifestyle Lessons

1. Remain inquisitive and curious! When you stop learning, you stop living.

2. Always "put your best foot forward." Be alert and truly interested in those around you and what they have to share and teach you.

3. Remember, you've lived this long without too many big mistakes. Be confident that you've learned something along the way.

4. Don't forget the saying: "The ones you've passed on the way up the ladder...are the same ones you'll pass coming down."

5. Successful women are open to change and able to recognize opportunities to support as well as learn from one another.

Today's career choices for women are better than ever. Were I fifty years younger, I'd find it very exciting, though a bit challenging, to select just one direction. Opportunities for those interested in following or creating an idea, in taking risks and, as ever, being willing to work are more vast than in years before. Diversity issues are front and center; gender bias — while still a contentious topic — is often forgotten in the maelstrom of sexual orientation issues and racial confusion. Capable individuals of all backgrounds and persuasions are receiving opportunities simply not available in previous times.

Accepting the Community Star Award from the Junior League of Sacramento in 2011.

When challenged about my perspective, I simply refer to my "Crayola View of Life": every picture is made better, more exciting and more complete by using the biggest box of crayons. The greater the diversity (of color, experience, belief, orientation, etc.), the better the picture as well as the ultimate success of the finished piece.

PATRICIA NICOSON

CIVIC ACTIVIST AND URBAN PLANNER — CHANGING PEOPLE'S LIVES

The women of our class were much more interested in having careers. We were on the cusp of women becoming much more independent. Previously, the key was to get a diamond ring by the time a woman graduated. Then, birth control pills came along and women could feel more sexually liberated, partly by being able to control when they wanted to have a family.

I knew I wanted to be involved in projects that would change people's lives. That's why I majored in architecture, urban design and planning. I recognized physical planning could be very effective and succeed in changing and improving the quality of people's lives and promoting community.

Patricia McLaughlin Nicoson

My Early Years
I grew up on a farm in Marshallton, just outside of Wilmington, Del., and was lucky to spend my elementary school years there. My father was an officer in the Coast Guard. He commuted to work in Philadelphia, did a tour in the Pacific, and came back to Philadelphia. The family was able to stay in Wilmington for eight years.

Although baptized a Roman Catholic, my mother said she was agnostic. She grew up in Brooklyn Heights, N. Y., and thought the nicest girls she knew went to "nuns' schools." So, she enrolled my sister, Elizabeth McLaughlin Poveromo, and me in Ursuline Academy in downtown Wilmington. I attended from first to eighth grades. When my father was transferred to Washington, D.C., I went to high school at Ursuline Academy in Bethesda, Md. There were only 27 girls in my high school class. I was the best in math and science, and very interested in biology and chemistry. A career in science was my initial goal.

My mother left college a month before she was to graduate from Connecticut College to marry my father. It was war time, 1941, so my mother didn't think she needed the degree. Although she never had a career, she was quite an active and independent woman as a stay-at-home mom. She also was active in the Republican Party and volunteered for a lot of other activities. My father left my education decisions to my mother and me. It was expected my three brothers, my sister and I would go to college. While my father's parents were college educated, my mother's were not.

My maternal grandmother was quite independent. She had been a partner with my grandfather in a developing a successful business, operating a rendering plant. (Rendering plants process animal by-product materials to produce tallow, grease, and high-protein meat and bone meal. We benefited from one byproduct, lanolin soaps, for many years.) Their first plant in Brooklyn was bought by the government to make room for the Brooklyn Queens Expressway. They then moved to Wilmington and built and operated a rendering plant there. I was fortunate to have had two outstanding female role models in my family — my mother and grandmother — who were independent and gutsy.

Because I had attended an all-girls school and lived on a farm for eight years, I wanted to go to a coed college in a big city. The nuns offered a scholarship to the College of New Rochelle in New York, and I had considered Bryn Mawr College in Pennsylvania, but both were all-girls schools. I wanted to attend a co-educational college. After receiving a scholarship from the University of Pennsylvania, my interests and the financing assistance lined up, and I went to Penn.

My Penn Experience
When I got into Penn, we were told we were "the best and the brightest ever to come along." We were smart; most were near or at the top of their class. Very few women (385) were accepted at Penn in 1960.

I've always been an activist. As a freshman, I helped create "Renaissance," a small group that wanted to create forums to discuss significant issues and ideas. We held one forum that I was involved in planning. We thought we were going to change the world. I participated in Bennett Union (for women) activities and served on the board my senior year. My best friends during my first two years at Penn had been upperclassmen. I missed them when they graduated. Although I didn't join a sorority in my first two years at Penn, friends in Kappa Kappa Gamma urged me to join in my junior year. I did and enjoyed living with them in the sorority house and participating in the sorority group life. My senior year, I roomed with three other women in the sorority house; it was a different and good experience for me.

In my first semester as a chemistry major, I was the only woman taking classes in chemistry, calculus, German and English for engineers. Although my grades were fine, a future as a chemist was not for me. In my sophomore year, I switched my major to architecture. I was always good in geometry and solid geometry — as a kid I designed play houses — so I was following a natural path.

My degree is a Bachelor of Arts with a major in Architecture. The class of 1963 was the last class to go through the five-year undergraduate program to receive a Bachelor of Architecture. Most of the students who wanted to be architects went on to graduate school to get the degree they needed. In the 1960s, architecture was viewed as a man's profession, but I didn't feel any discrimination in class as a woman.

Penn had a great, highly regarded architecture school and planning department. I studied with very intelligent students and had outstanding, inspiring teachers, including the revered Louis Kahn, Denise Scott Brown, Robert Venturi and Ian McHarg. Although I was an undergraduate, I was able to take courses with them in the graduate school.

Later, when I took a job at the Washington, D.C., Office of Planning in 1976, I met Marilyn Jordan Taylor of Skidmore Owings and Merrill (SOM). She was co-leader of the Mayor's Blue Ribbon Committee on the Downtown, and I was a Downtown D.C. planner, also working on the plan during Mayor Marion Barry's administration. Taylor was an inspiration for women who were interested in the field of architecture and urban design. She recently retired as Dean of the Penn School of Architecture.

Among the 80 architecture students, there were only three other women in my classes. There was no discussion in the classroom or in seminars about women in the workplace. A "dress code" was never an issue for me. At Ursuline Academy, we wore nylon stockings and uniforms — a blazer and a pleated skirt. At Penn, I always wore stockings and skirts, and I still wear pantyhose to this day. I never wore pants as a student or professional until I started to work in 1998 as President of the Dulles Corridor Rail Association, located in Reston, Va.

Furthering My Education
I hoped a planning career would give me an opportunity to improve people's lives. At Penn, I was exposed to great architecture and urban planning and saw what good architecture and urban design could do for the quality of life and people's experiences. Philadelphia was undergoing a planning renaissance that encompassed many sections of the downtown area, including historic Society Hill, which was being renovated. There were so many good architects working in the city that they were referred to as the "Philadelphia School." I could also see how

the evolving design of the Penn campus promoted interaction among people and inspired conversing and collaboration.

In August of 1965, I married William Todd Fairbairn, III, who had studied at Hamilton College and graduated from Penn. We moved to Manhattan. My husband worked for IBM. "Now what am I going to do?" I asked myself. Because my BA with a major in architecture didn't qualify me as an architect, and I didn't fancy being a starving architectural draftsman, I decided to investigate planning. I had been exposed to great planning at Penn, both in the city of Philadelphia and in my planning courses at Penn. The answer was graduate school at Pratt Institute in Brooklyn. It seemed like a good career opportunity.

As it happened, Mary Hommann, the vice chair of the City and Regional Planning Department at Pratt Institute, was an early graduate of Penn's planning program and became a leader in the field. I was accepted into the program at Pratt in January 1966 and took classes there for two years. Subsequently, I served for several semesters as a teaching assistant in the introductory planning design course.

In January 1969, my son, William Todd Fairbairn, IV, was born, followed by daughter Mary Cameron Fairbairn (now Morgan) in March 1970. When the children were small, I stayed at home and worked on a handbook for Pratt's Planning Design course. To keep my brain engaged, I took courses at the New School. One was "New Town Planning," which focused on the planning and construction of English and French new towns, and the construction of Reston, Virginia, and Columbia, Maryland, in the United States, which were then underway. The course was taught by Bob Simon, Reston's developer, and Bill Nicoson, the first Administrator of the New Communities Program at the Department of Housing and Urban Development.

My husband received a promotion from IBM and we moved to Washington, D.C. in 1974, living in the Dupont Circle area. The next year, I finished my thesis on the new town of Columbia,, Md., and received my M.S. degree in city and regional planning from Pratt.

With my daughter, son and grandchildren, April 2017.

156

I joined a small group of citizens beginning to plan for the Dupont Circle area. In the early 1970s, skyscrapers were marching up Connecticut Avenue, threatening the historic buildings. We succeeded in getting Marion Barry, who was running to become the first elected mayor of Washington, D.C., to support our plans for downzoning the Dupont Circle area.

The decision by my husband and me to purchase a five-story town house in Dupont Circle was helpful in securing good child care. The house had a bedroom on the fifth floor that was used by au pairs at first, and then by college students who helped with the children. Besides providing room and board, we paid them a modest stipend. By the time I started to work full time, my children attended Sidwell Friends, in nearby Bethesda, Md., on a full day schedule. The au pairs or students met them after school and took care of them until I came home from work. Our Dupont Circle location, close to downtown D.C. with its shops and universities, proved an asset in hiring child care help.

In 1975, my husband and I separated. I reconnected with Bill Nicoson from the New Town Planning course at the New School. He was working as an urban affairs expert in private practice. I met with Bill to seek help with connections to potential employers. No referrals were forthcoming, but he and I began dating, culminating in our marriage in 1986 and my move to Reston.

My Career
My first planning job, in 1969, was working for Mary Hommann after she left Pratt and became planning director of Yonkers, N.Y. I worked for her for about nine months before Bill Fairbairn and I moved to Washington. Serving as a planner in Yonkers was an important addition to my resume. Mary is still a close friend.

My first job in Washington began in 1974, as a part-time teaching assistant in the Department of Urban and Regional Planning at George Washington University (GWU) in D.C. I did not encounter any discrimination against women. The Department staff was delighted to have me join them. For several years, I helped teach an Urban Design Course — Planning 101 — and the History of Planning course.

In 1976, I started to work for the District of Columbia full-time as a Community Planner, focusing on planning projects for the Downtown and Dupont Circle areas. One of my major projects was to lead the planning effort to rezone the Dupont Circle area, a long and complicated case involving thousands of properties. The first phase of Metrorail had opened in 1976, and the Dupont Circle station was the interim end of the line. At the same time, Dupont Circle was designated an historic district.

Rezoning involved downzoning properties along Connecticut and Massachusetts Avenues, NW, as well as other streets, which protected the historic structures and encouraged a mix of uses. Mayor Barry had committed to supporting the citizens' plan for Dupont Circle. I was pleased to be the planner to successfully present the zoning case to the D.C. Zoning Commission. Another major project I led was the creation of a one-step Planned Unit Development process that enabled a developer to expedite the rezoning of a project meeting certain requirements. Later I worked as the Downtown (Ward 2) planner.

Mayor Barry issued a call to his employees saying, "I'd like to hear what's on your mind. Give me some of your suggestions and I'll pick the best." I was selected to meet with the Mayor and gave him my ideas for a Blue Ribbon Commission which could bring together the various constituents in the city to work on a plan for rehabilitating the dilapidated downtown between Union Station and the White House. Mayor Barry liked the suggestion, and created the Mayor's Downtown Committee.

That's when I met Marilyn Jordan Taylor, subsequently Dean of the School of Architecture at Penn, because she was one of the high-level professionals who helped the Mayor develop this Blue Ribbon plan for the Living Downtown. By that time, I had moved to the Department of Transportation. Another staffer and I in the Planning Division were working on Downtown streetscape, urban design and public space issues, so we were major participants in this planning effort. Taylor, who at the time worked at Skidmore Owings and Merrill, was a key person in moving the Downtown plan forward to completion.

Although more women were coming into the workplace, feminism and glass ceilings were not concepts I remember hearing about in college. They certainly were there when I started to work for the District. While I did not feel discrimination in getting jobs at the time, priority in the D.C. Office of Planning was put on bringing in and promoting African Americans. I changed departments to advance.

In 1980, I joined the D.C. Department of Transportation at a higher-grade level. Most of the department heads in the government were white. Mayor Barry replaced these department heads with his own people. Barry did bring in some women in senior positions and as heads of departments. One example was Carol Thompson Cole, who was head of the Department of Housing and Community Development. She wasn't trained for this role, but she was smart and politically well-connected and did well. She was another good role model.

In my six years (1980 to 1986) at the Department of Transportation as a transportation planner with land use expertise, there were some successes and some setbacks. My most challenging assignment was as project manager for the Barney Circle Study, a preliminary engineering and Environmental Impact Study (EIS) financed with the District's last remaining Interstate Highway funding.

The Barney Circle Study examined alternatives to link the Southeast Freeway with the Anacostia Freeway across the Anacostia River. It was a key missing link in the freeway system. The engineering study and the EIS were completed successfully with citizen support. The residents of the Capitol Hill neighborhood at the time were opposed to the significant volumes of peak period traffic that traveled through their neighborhood daily. The Freeway link across the Anacostia River would have taken traffic out of their neighborhood. Even though it achieved the necessary local and federal approvals, Barney Circle never was completed. Major highway projects fell out of popular favor.

The Department of Transportation was reorganized as the Department of Public Works (DPW). The new director replaced many of the previous division and department heads with minority employees. The woman who headed the Office of Transportation Planning where I worked, Sarah Campbell, had formerly worked in the office of the U.S. Secretary of Transportation and was extremely capable and well-equipped to handle this very complicated job. She was an excellent role model for me and the other two professional women in the Planning Division. Her obvious competence and leadership skills won the respect of the male leadership in the Department.

As chair of the Downtown Streetscape Committee at DPW, I headed the team that reviewed all development plans to make sure the trees, landscaping and street paving that we selected for the Downtown were installed. I developed a proposal for an Urban Design and Transportation study to complement the Downtown plan. Up to one million dollars from the Urban Mass Transit Administration was secured to fund it.

However, I became disillusioned by the way in which the government handled the project. The day before the proposals were due, my boss told me that not only would I not chair the consultant team selection committee, I would not even serve on it.

The Downtown Urban Design and Transportation study would have been an important project for the District to undertake. The contract required transportation expertise and urban design credentials. But the selected contractor lacked staff with the backgrounds and experience to produce usable recommendations. Originally, it did not even have a transportation consultant as part of the team. In the end, to my disappointment, the District spent nearly $250,000 on the project before it was terminated with no usable results.

Although I loved my work, I realized it was time to leave District employment. In May 1986, I became a senior transportation planner with Arlington, Va., which at the time was considered the epitome of good government. In 1988, I was elected President of the National Capital Area Chapter of the American Planning Association (APA).

As President of the APA chapter, I formed a coalition of four groups (APA, the Committee of 100 on the Federal City, the Historic Preservation League and the Downtown Cluster of Congregations) to bring the Downtown Plan to the D.C. Zoning Commission. Because no zoning had been adopted to support the Downtown plan, the city was not achieving its goals while property owners and developers were reaping great financial rewards. I spent nights and weekends for nearly two years developing the Downtown Development District zoning plan recommendations with other coalition members and brought it to the Zoning Commission, testifying numerous times. The major achievement of the plan was to promote housing development downtown to achieve the "Living Downtown." The zoning plan also supported mixed use, theaters and other cultural resources, historic preservation and affordable housing.

While I was leading the presentation of the zoning case as head of APA, I was still working full-time for Arlington County. I was the senior professional woman in the Public Works Department and I was only a grade 12. DPW had no women in management, and only years after I started was an African American man appointed as a Division head. Our department received special attention from the County Manager who provided consultants to work with the management team and employees to change the culture and leadership style.

Because I was the senior woman, I was involved with all the diversity training sessions with the men who headed up the five different divisions. I created a woman's group after one of these sessions, because it was pitifully obvious that the value of women wasn't being recognized. Then, using bagels as a lure, I began holding staff meetings for our Division. After six months, the staff recognized the value of these meetings, and we agreed to rotate leadership of the meetings. I initiated brown bag lunches to share information among the various divisions. Later, I organized interdepartmental lunches, featuring department heads sharing information about major projects. All this was new to Arlington.

The elected officials, the Arlington County Board members, were wonderful—topnotch, exemplary people, many of whom went on to higher leadership positions in the state. Because my division was so small, I had many different responsibilities. I represented the county on the Transportation Planning Board Technical Committee of the Metropolitan Washington Council of Governments, chairing it for six months before I retired. I represented the county on transportation policy issues at the state level and lobbied frequently in Richmond. I also managed the capital budget for transportation projects and led neighborhood traffic planning efforts.

I was sent to Kepner Trego project management and decision-making courses. With the knowledge gained, I worked with the Human Resources staff person to create a project management course, which I co-taught, for employees of the Department. I also was the Project Manager of the North Quincy Extension project, a six-year effort that began with working with six civic associations to develop the plan, overseeing the engineering and finally the construction of the new street, a two-block project in the middle of Ballston. The project went through a Metro bus parking garage, so it involved building demolition, property acquisitions, and ground water and asbestos remediation. Instead of handing projects off to different divisions as was the practice, the Department leadership wanted to have a project manager for the life of the project. By having one-person familiar with and responsible for all phases of the project, the project was able to move forward more quickly.

Retirement. Well, That Didn't Happen.
Even though I received many awards, I really didn't feel my career was advancing. After 12 years, I realized there was just no place for me to go, and I decided to leave. At 55, I could officially retire.

I had always been a civic activist in Reston, heading the Transportation Committee for several years. I became chair of the Reston Metrorail Access Group, which worked with a consultant to develop recommendations for transportation improvements to support pedestrian, bicycle, transit and vehicular access to the four Metrorail stations in and near Reston. Its success spawned similar groups for the Tysons and Herndon transit station areas. As Chairperson of the Reston Master Plan Special Study Committee, I coordinated a four-year effort of a 25-member group (plus 25 alternates) to develop recommendations for the land uses and densities around the three Metrorail stations in Reston.

In addition to good quality architecture, contributions to the transportation system, parks and cultural facilities, the plan required 20 percent affordable workforce housing. That meant we had to overturn covenants that restricted housing along much of the Dulles corridor. The planning approach was new in that it did not specify uses for individual parcels but rather larger subareas. Staff could negotiate with developers to provide density in exchange for the desired amenities. The plan was widely supported by the community. They had seen the success of the Reston Town Center, a high-density, mixed-use downtown of Reston and were not afraid of density so long as the appropriate transportation and community facilities were provided along with development.

I was familiar with the Dulles Corridor Metrorail Project, which had been on the books for many years. The median of the 23-mile Dulles Toll Road/Dulles International Airport Access Highway (a superhighway from Washington, D.C., to Washington Dulles International Airport) was reserved for a transit link when Dulles Airport was planned, but none was ever built. Virginia House

Receiving the Tower of Dulles Award from the Committee for Dulles, 2015.

of Delegates member Ken Plum canvassed community and business leaders and decided the best thing to do would be to create a single-focus organization that would champion bringing the Metrorail system out the Dulles corridor to the Airport and into Loudoun County.

Working on extending Metrorail in the Dulles corridor was too hard to resist. Having been immersed in land use and transportation planning, I said, "Well, here I am, recently retired, I can be president." That was just four months after I left Arlington government, and I held that title for 18 years until the end of 2016. The creation of the Dulles Corridor Rail Association (DCRA) was announced at a press conference in Reston on August 3, 1998. In January 2017, DCRA declared, "Mission Accomplished" and merged with the Northern Virginia Transportation Alliance.

DCRA was a non-profit, 501(c)(4) organization. It was basically me as a one-person shop, with part-time help on the website and bookkeeping. The mission was to build public support for the Metrorail extension and advise decision makers on rail-related issues. I lobbied at the federal, state, and local levels to get funding and approvals for the Dulles Metrorail Project. For four years, funding for my minimal salary was largely raised by me personally. Fortunately, with better financial support, my earnings improved considerably. I communicated with members with daily emails, fact sheets and newsletters, ran seminars, served on four chambers of commerce policy committees, and was on the boards of several business organizations, including the Dulles Area Transportation Association. My role was as champion and liaison to this major project—a $5.8 billion Metrorail extension serving the major activity centers of Tysons, Reston, Herndon, Washington Dulles International Airport and eastern Loudoun.

 The first 13-mile phase from West Falls Church to Reston East opened in July 2015. The second phase is well underway and will be open for operations in the spring of 2020. Ridership has been less than projected, due mainly to an extensive repair program undertaken by the Washington Metropolitan Area Transportation Association that has closed segments of the entire system for more than a year (2016-2017), causing major delays. However, there are more than 20 mixed-use development projects underway in Tysons and 13 in Reston that will bring employees and residents to work and live along the Metrorail line (now called the Silver line) that will generate substantial increases in ridership.

Metrorail is a powerful economic development generator. During 2015, 92 percent of all commercial leasing took place within one-half mile of the Metrorail. Employers and developers recognize that younger workers want to be in a mixed use, transit-accessible environment.

For me, there was no more important project in the country than linking our National Capital with Dulles International Airport and six major activity centers along the way. I also welcomed the opportunity to get involved in a project that addressed social justice issues such as affordable housing and access to jobs, as well as educational, health and cultural facilities, and quality of life issues including protection of the environment, lower costs of living through reducing the need to own vehicles, and the provision of life style choices.

Giving Back
As it turns out, no interest is ever wasted. I'm now on the Advisory Board of the Children's Science Center (CSC). We have a "Lab" facility at Fair Oaks Mall, Fairfax County, Va. We do our best to attract young

people up to the age of 14 to take an interest in STEM (science technology, engineering and math). Planning is underway to develop a $30 million first-phase Science Museum in eastern Loudoun. The governor of Virginia appointed me to the Board of Trustees of the Science Museum of Virginia in Richmond, Va. The CSC board is working to develop a relationship with the state museum.

I am also on the Associates Board of the Wolf Trap National Park for the Performing Arts, known locally in the Washington, D.C. area simply as Wolf Trap. It also has an Early Childhood Educational Institute that seeks to put the Arts in STEM — thereby generating STEAM — by training teachers, not only in Virginia but also throughout the United States and in several locations abroad, on how to incorporate dance, movement and the arts to develop an understanding of scientific principles. I am also on the boards of the George Washington chapter of Lambda Alpha International (an honorary land economics society), and the Fairfax County Committee of 100.

Advice to Students
I have never spoken to future Penn graduates, but I would like to say:

The motto of my high school, Ursuline Academy, was "Serviam," Latin for "I will serve." The Ursuline education incorporated service into the learning process. I viewed becoming a planner as a way to serve the community and gravitated to public service for employment. Civic activity shaped my career path. I became involved in things I cared about, like planning for my Dupont Circle neighborhood.

Getting involved as a citizen in the Dupont Circle project and in Reston transportation issues led to employment and the ability to effect change. Although I didn't have a planned-out career path, opportunities came as a result of my interest in improving my communities.

Follow your passion, your interests. Keep your eyes open, look around. There are always opportunities to make improvements in your communities. The ability to feel like you are having an impact on people's lives is important for you and for those who benefit from your contribution.

ANDREA PILCH

FROM POLITICAL SCIENCE MAJOR TO INVESTMENT MANAGER

I was never an activist in the women's movement. I didn't know anyone who went out and picketed or protested, although I cared deeply about this issue. I always felt that I was part of the women's movement in my own way. It did not pass me by.

Andrea Pilch

My Early Education and Penn Decision
Graduating first in my class of 476 students at Germantown High School carried a tremendous perk: a Philadelphia Mayor's Scholarship which provided full tuition to Penn for four years. I had always wanted to go to Penn because I perceived it as a "campus" school rather than a stop on the subway. It was like a dream to be able to attend an Ivy League university.

Originally, I had been accepted to Penn's School of Education because in 1960 everyone figured that a "girl" would become a teacher. Then I saw the array of Wharton courses in Penn's catalog, and I knew that a business career was what really interested me. The Wharton School curriculum held much more appeal than teaching and, before my freshman year started, I switched to Wharton.

My father was the administrative assistant in Philadelphia to U.S. Senator Hugh Scott of Pennsylvania. Not surprisingly, political science was my chosen major rather than finance (which would be my future investment career). With my father working for the Senator, I always thought I would end up in government. I did a summer internship in the Senator's Washington, D.C., office and found it fascinating. However I also was somewhat disillusioned. Being in Washington didn't feel like being in the real world, but almost seemed like being in an ivory tower.

My greatest interests always were in history and politics, two areas that my father loved as well. He was a strong influence on my life and education. Both my parents instilled in me the values and ethical standards I have observed throughout my life. I always wanted to excel and I did, graduating *cum laude* from Penn. In my junior year, I was inducted into Beta Gamma Sigma, the premier honor society recognizing academic excellence at Wharton.

My Penn Experience

Penn was a whole new world for me. While I excelled in high school, when I arrived at Penn I found that everyone else had done so as well. Many had been editors-in-chief of their high school newspapers, as I had been, or president of their student council. We had been big fish in little ponds and then became little fish in a big pond! It also was a world of people from all different economic backgrounds from all over the country.

I never took trips on spring breaks, and worked during summer vacations. I am forever grateful for the scholarship that enabled me to attend Penn, the wonderful contacts I made, and the outstanding education I received. Having the degree from the Wharton School at Penn meant everything.

There were only twelve women in my freshman Wharton class. (As a side note, I remember that women were supposed to wear skirts rather than slacks to class.) With the first two years of basic core courses set for everyone, you chose your major in your junior year. I also found there was ample room for the electives I really wanted to take, such as music and history. Even though I was in Wharton, I wasn't restricted to all business courses.

My favorite Penn professor was Dr. Henry J. Abraham in Wharton's political science department. I helped proofread the fourth edition of his book, *Elements of Democratic Government,* and was noted in the preface as one of his research assistants. I especially remember his outstanding constitutional law course. My senior thesis for Wharton, which I still have, was titled "The Nuremberg Trials, Some Legal Aspects." Dr. Abraham and I corresponded for many years after Penn about my career, politics and life in general.

My Career Begins

When I graduated, the business climate was not really an open environment for women, although it changed dramatically over the years. I was among the first women to join The Bond Club of Philadelphia and The Philadelphia Securities Association. I also belonged to The Financial Analysts of Philadelphia.

In the spring semester of my senior year, I interviewed with recruiters on the Penn campus and accepted a position at Citibank in New York City. Since I lived and went to college in Philadelphia, I wanted to move to the Big Apple to work. I was placed in Citibank's trust investment training program. Most valuable was my introduction to the fundamentals of municipal bonds, always one of my favorite areas of the bond market, both personally and professionally. I also spent time doing basic equity investment research. The Citibank experience gave me an excellent foundation, but I realized that I didn't want to be a full-time research analyst.

When I left Citibank, I made a detour from investments and joined the Wage and Hour Division of the U.S. Department of Labor. It was not a good move as I was visiting offices and sweat shops in Manhattan, checking on compliance issues. I saw a slice of another world during that experience. It was a real eye opener, and I regretted leaving Citibank and finance.

Making and finding close friends was difficult in New York City. I missed my family and friends in Philadelphia and decided to return home. With my Wharton and Citibank background, several job offers came my way. I joined the Fidelity Mutual Life Insurance Company where I worked on private placements and other bond-related programs. I was earning a higher salary than in my original job at Citibank and didn't feel any discrimination as a woman, although I had never felt any discrimination at Citibank either.

With a business colleague, Rachel Perlman, who hosted my retirement party.

I spent five years in the investment advisory department of Drexel Burnham Lambert, working on fixed income investments for a corporate bond fund and a broad variety of other accounts. The job involved a substantial amount of bond trading in an era before we had sophisticated computer equipment and the Bloomberg technology services. However, with the guidance of a marvelous boss, my years at Drexel were probably the most significant in sharpening my overall bond investment expertise.

Along the way, I made another detour, but not from investments. For a short time, I worked on the investment portfolio of an insurance company in Miami and lived on beautiful Key Biscayne. However, the investment community in Miami was considerably less sophisticated than in Philadelphia or New York. I was offered a bond management position at a bank in Atlanta, but the lure of family and friends in Philadelphia again won the day. I returned home and eventually landed at The Bryn Mawr Trust Company, one of the best job moves I ever made.

I ended my career as a senior vice president at Bryn Mawr Trust, where I had spent seventeen years. I worked in the trust and investment division, where I managed our four bond common trust funds as well as investments in personal trust and advisory accounts. I made many wonderful friendships at Bryn Mawr Trust that are still very special in retirement. From a financial point of view, I was fortunate that the firm had a defined benefit pension plan, a definite plus!

Business Relationships
Penn didn't teach us about networking, but I had my Rolodex of contacts which was invaluable for help in changing jobs. I learned about networking "on the job."

I always endeavored to do my best and was treated with respect by my co-workers. Good relationships were of the utmost importance to me. I was considerate of the people who were above and below me in the organizational hierarchy. My parents taught me to treat everyone equally. In my various jobs, I often noted people being demanding and rude to support staff and colleagues. That was never my style.

Retirement – Still Active and Involved
I retired from Bryn Mawr Trust on Valentine's Day in 2003 and moved to Sarasota, Florida, where I had purchased a villa the prior year. I vowed never to see snow again!

My father, a widower since 1982, moved to an excellent retirement residence in Sarasota at the same time to be near his only child. We both made many good friends in our new community and had many special times together until he passed away in 2008.

I became actively involved in my homeowners association shortly after I arrived in Sarasota and have served on

With my father.

the Board of Directors since I moved there. I was president for five years in a row and have been the association treasurer for many years as well. Fortunately, we have an excellent management company which eases the burden of Board membership, since it is often difficult to find volunteers to run for the Board.

My Commitment to Education
My special local philanthropic cause is The Education Foundation of Sarasota County, which provides funds for numerous outstanding initiatives and special programs for students and teachers that are either beyond or not covered by the regular Sarasota school system budget. My

commitment to this organization and education in general can be attributed to my gratitude to the teachers who taught me and the foundation they gave me to succeed in life.

Even more significant for me is supporting education by endowing scholarships. I have endowed a scholarship in my name at Penn and another in my parents' name at Temple University in the Fox School of Business. My father was a 1937 Temple graduate. Setting up the scholarships is one of the best things I've ever done. It has been a most fulfilling experience to get to know my "scholars." They are dynamic individuals, and I am very proud of them.

Reflecting

Looking back, I believe I always worked to the best of my ability throughout my career, in good times and bad. I was fortunate to retire comfortably to my new life in Florida while young enough to enjoy it.

With classmates Anne Sceia Klein and Alan Rachins at our 25th Penn reunion.

BARBARA WONG, M.D.

A DISTINGUISHED CAREER IN MEDICINE

The women who graduated from Penn in 1964 had to be tough and determined to reach their goals in a male-dominated workplace. One had to be highly motivated and laser-focused to succeed. These qualities were fostered during my time at the College for Women at Penn but originated from my upbringing in the hardscrabble town of Chester, Pa.

Although now retired, I reflect on the fact that I practiced through the golden age of radiology and that I, and the excellent cadre of radiologists around me, have had a lasting impact on both the science of medicine and the community.

Barbara Schepps Wong, MD

The Foundation: Early Life Lessons

My father, Melvin Schepps, was born in 1908 in Poland, growing up there during the First World War. His formal education was limited, and life for the Jews in Poland was difficult. In his twenties, he emigrated to Palestine where he worked as a laborer. In 1938, sponsored by his uncle Henry, he emigrated to New York City where he was introduced to my mother, Rose Witlin, by mutual relatives. My parents settled in Chester, Pa., near my maternal grandparents, Annie and Samuel Witlin, both of whom had emigrated to the U.S. at the turn of the century.

My mother, Rose (Witlin) Schepps, and her sister, Eva, and brother, Morton, attended public schools, all graduating at the tops of their classes. For financial reasons, neither of these women went to college. My uncle later went to Temple University on the GI bill. He owned a retail business. Both my mother and her sister worked as bookkeepers before marriage.

I was an only child and my father believed that a wife was meant to keep house and care for her family, so my mother did not work outside the home until I was in high school. My father's first job was filling vending machines, for which he made $15.00 a week. Because of his lack of education, he had a series of unskilled jobs. We lived in a three-room apartment until I was 13, when we moved to a small house in a better part of Chester. My father's uncle lived with us. My parents wanted a different life for me, and education was the key to achieving that goal. They instilled a strong work ethic in me.

From the age of 13, I worked in my uncle's grocery store as a cashier and stock girl each day after school and on Saturdays. My uncle was a hard taskmaster. In my spare time, I babysat and did some lifeguarding at a summer day camp.

From an early age, my life goal was to become a physician. Science was one of my first loves, and it would ultimately lead me to a career in medicine. My wish was to help people and to make a positive difference in their lives. That sounds simplistic today but that's how I felt I could do the most good. I didn't realize it at the time, but I was beginning to set and accomplish a series of goals that gave me ownership of my future. I learned to become self-reliant. During several summers, I worked in a hospital lab. My objective to become a medical doctor was furthered by my admiration for the physicians I encountered there.

Penn State Fails, Penn Succeeds

Chester High School was not a top-rated institution. Although there were some wonderful teachers, it was an institution that sent only a minority of its graduates to a college of any sort. There was little counseling and the education was average at best. I had to develop my own exit strategy. We looked for an affordable college, and I ended up at Pennsylvania State University. I spent my freshman year at the campus in State College, Pa.

Penn State was not for me. I was there to get an education and not to party or meet a prospective husband. I loathed Penn State from the moment I set foot there. Class sizes were humongous, instructors were remote, and having a good time was most important for the majority. If I were studying, my dorm mates would laugh at me. I'm sure they wondered why I wasn't like them, out partying and going for my MRS. It also irked me that a football player friend of mine got the chemistry test questions and answers before the exams.

I had to get out of Penn State. My parents were sending me a meager allowance because I couldn't get a campus job as a freshman. Transferring to Penn would put me in a better academic environment, and there would be more opportunities for employment. So, I made the decision to apply and was thrilled when I was accepted for my sophomore year. A whole new world was opening up to me.

From my first steps on campus, I directed my education at Penn to my dream of becoming a physician. I knew that women doctors were still a scarcity, so I prepared myself for an extended challenge. Penn awarded me some financial aid, and I was able to land a job in a research lab at the Hospital of the University of Pennsylvania doing grunt work to subsidize my living expenses. I was working hard and enjoyed the course work. I loved Penn for giving this opportunity to advance my future goals. Then, things started to fall into place.

Classes at Penn were so much better: they were smaller, and the instructors knew you. My career goals were so focused that I missed out on the other aspects of campus life. It was only at my 50th Reunion that I learned that one of my classmates, both at Penn and later at Hahnemann, was an all-Ivy quarterback for Penn. I never saw a football game at Penn. I worked a lot. What else did I miss?

Beginning a Medical Career
Chemistry was my major. One of the professors, Dr. Madeline Jolliet, really cared about women's education and was very kind. Majoring in chemistry also fulfilled many of the pre-med requirements. I also took the opportunity to explore courses in art history and social science. I loved Penn and the diversity of its student body, and even the chilly nights my first year living in Sargent Hall!

My next challenge was getting into medical school. I knew that, as a woman, it would be a difficult task. I would be in a minority. In 1963, with the exception of those at Women's Medical College of Pennsylvania, there were generally fewer than 10 percent women in medical school classes. A female applicant was less likely to get an interview, even when compared with male applicants with lower credentials and fewer qualifications. When Hahnemann Medical College (as it was known then) accepted me, I was extraordinarily pleased to be admitted. Of the 110 students in my class, 10 were women. Of course, now half or more of most med school classes are composed of women.

To help make ends meet at Hahnemann, one of my jobs was working in the Emergency Department for 12 hours each Saturday and Sunday as a clerk admitting patients. My medical school colleague worked the night shift and I worked the day. In the summer, a female neuro-anatomy professor mentored many of us females by giving us work in her research lab. My work ethic sustained me.

I met my husband, Richard Wong, who was a class ahead of me at Hahnemann. He became a general and vascular surgeon. We got married the week after I graduated, then moved to Boston. I did my internship in Medicine at New England Deaconess and my residency in Radiology at Boston City Hospital. Of the nine who were in my residency year, I was the only woman. There were four women out of a total of 27 residents in the radiology program. I had chosen radiology because I planned to have a family and wanted a job with fixed hours. That turned out to be fantasy. That's not what radiology was then and far from what it is now. It certainly wasn't what my career would ultimately become.

Radiology would evolve from just interpreting plain x-rays and doing barium studies to deploying revolutionary developments including CT scanning, magnetic resonance imaging (MRI), and catheter intervention both for diagnosis and treatment. The myth of not having interaction with patients was just a myth, particularly for those of us doing interventional work and breast imaging.

My first day of internship at New England Deaconess Hospital in Boston, 1968. I'm in the front row, third from right.

The first day of residency, the nine of us were ushered into a conference room to hear a talk by the chief x-ray technician. I was very pregnant, not a good way to start a radiology residency. He looked around the room and then said, in a loud voice, "There are two places where a woman belongs. One is the kitchen." He was not the first nor the last misogynist I would encounter in my medical career.

Everyone else, especially my fellow residents, were extraordinarily kind and caring. The schedule was worked so that I did not have to get irradiated during my pregnancy. Our daughter, Debbie (Penn '91, University of Pittsburgh Medical School '97 and currently an emergency room physician at Mount Auburn Hospital in Cambridge, Mass.), was born by Caesarian section. I was allowed to use my entire month of vacation as maternity leave. How far we've come! While my husband worked every other night and every other weekend, I was lucky to work only one night a week.

As an intern, my husband made $3,000 a year, jumping to $6,000 a year during residency. I made slightly more. Because the nanny earned about as much as one of our salaries per year, Richard moonlighted every third weekend in a local ER. He basically had one weekend off a month. I did the billing so he could get paid. We were still poor, but I was happy.

When residencies were completed, Richard (and I) had to deal with the Vietnam War. All male med school grads owed military service. Richard was lucky to be able to complete his surgical residency before serving, and he was stationed at Lockbourne Air Force Base in Columbus, Ohio. I secured a job as a radiologist at Ohio State University. The daily commute was an hour each way, and I worked three days each week. I felt fortunate to get a great job working in a fine academic radiology department.

With my husband, Richard.

However, I came to learn I was being paid on a different pay scale than my male peers. Women and foreign male doctors were paid less. With some trepidation, I decided to discuss this with my boss, the chief of radiology, and he did agree to revise the system. With this encounter, I had learned to speak up. I had made a difference, and this discriminatory practice was ended for everyone.

Despite my not attending any football games at Penn, football games were a large part of life at OSU. I had access to good seats through my work. Football was *THE* social event of the fall season in Columbus, and it was fun to be in that environment. While my experience in Columbus was positive, Richard and I both wanted to return to the East Coast to practice our specialties and to raise our daughter.

A Stroke of Luck
After the military, Richard was offered a job with a group of surgeons in Rhode Island with whom he had worked during residency. We were thrilled to be returning to the East Coast. My job would be a little more difficult to come by, as there were only two practicing female radiologists in the whole state of Rhode Island at the time. You can

imagine my astonishment when I received a letter from the chief of one of the radiology groups, stating that he would <u>NEVER</u> hire a woman radiologist because she wouldn't be able to "do everything." I was devastated.

But then I took advantage of a stroke of luck. A diagnostic radiology group called Ray Medical (now Rhode Island Medical Imaging) had formed a few years earlier in Providence. It was associated with Rhode Island Hospital and subsequently Brown Medical School. One of the two female radiologists in the state practiced in this group. I would become the third practicing female radiologist in Rhode Island. When I began my practice in Rhode Island, the residency program was solely hospital based; but as the Brown University Program in Medicine grew, the practice became a major part of the radiology faculty.

Shortly after I arrived, I was asked to be involved in a study sponsored by the National Cancer Institute and the American Cancer Society (The Breast Cancer Demonstration Project, BCDP). Its purpose was to determine if screening asymptomatic women with mammography would reduce breast cancer mortality. Rhode Island Hospital was one of the 27 study sites nationally. I became expert at interpreting screening mammograms. The study ran from 1974 to 1982 and demonstrated that screening asymptomatic women with annual mammography reduced breast cancer mortality for those who were screened.

The focus of my subsequent academic and clinical medical career was that of a breast imager. I became involved on the state level helping to organize public awareness regarding mammography and early detection of breast cancer. With the Department of Health, we developed a program to educate the public, insurance providers and physicians about the advantage of early detection. The program offered low-cost screening as well as free screening to those in need. This program changed the lives of many.

In 1994, I was able to convince Rhode Island Hospital to open a free-standing breast imaging center. That center, The Anne C. Pappas Center for Breast Imaging, was the first such center in Rhode Island and still flourishes today. It was my vision, and I was its director until retiring from practice in December 2008. I am proud the Center remains a center of excellence for breast imaging with state-of-the-art equipment, a hard working technical staff, and devoted and gratified patients.

Academically, I was a journal reviewer in breast imaging for various medical journals, and was author or co-author of more than 100 medical articles. I have been invited to speak locally, nationally and internationally. For many years, I was course director of our departmental annual symposium of diagnostic imaging, held each summer in Newport, R.I.

Other Involvements

In addition to academic and clinical responsibilities, it was important for me to participate in the politics of medicine and health policy. For our private practice radiology group, I served as president for 11 years, during which time we grew from 15 doctors to 45. I served on multiple committees at Rhode Island Hospital, Women and Infants Hospital, Brown Medical School and the Rhode Island Department of Health. I chaired the Credentials Committee at Rhode Island Hospital for six years. Other appointments included the Rhode Island Hospital Board of Trustees election as president of the Medical Staff, and president of the Rhode Island Radiological Society. In 1994, I was named president of the Rhode Island Medical Society, serving a one-year term.

At my induction as president of the Rhode Island Medical Society in 1994, with my daughter Debbie.

There were many honors I have been proud to receive, including a lifetime achievement award from the Rhode Island branch of the American Cancer Society. Academically, I've retired as Professor of Radiology, Clinical, at the Alpert School of Medicine at Brown University. The most gratifying professional recognition was having the Pappas Breast Imaging Center dedicated in my honor shortly before I retired.

Being focused and motivated allowed me to succeed in an arena where few women were afforded the privilege. Penn played a great part in my gaining self-confidence, and I am in debt to Penn for preparing me.

Although now retired, I reflect on the fact I practiced through the golden age of radiology and that I, and the excellent cadre of radiologists who were around me, left a lasting impact on both the science of medicine and the community.

In retrospect, I had a wonderful career and a charmed life as a practitioner in the noble profession of medicine. I now most enjoy spending time with my 6-year-old twin grandchildren, Chris and James. It is my dream that I will be able to instill my work ethic in them, and their lives will be happy and successful. Happily, they are showing signs

of the self-reliance that has sustained me. My hope is that they will have
the luck to go to college at a place as great as Penn.

Receiving the Lifetime Achievement Award from the Rhode
Island branch of the American Cancer Society.

A Professor's Perspectives on 50 Years

By Klaus Krippendorff
Professor Emeritus of Communication
The Annenberg School for Communication
University of Pennsylvania

In 2015, members of the Annenberg School for Communication's 1965 graduating class met in Philadelphia for their 50th reunion. This was only the fifth graduating class in the School's short history; there had never before been a reunion of this kind and none since. After serving on the University's 1964 reunion committee, Anne Klein chaired this Annenberg reunion.

I was most impressed by how many of these graduates made the considerable effort to come from all over the country to this event. To feel connected to one's alma mater after pursuing different professional paths says something about the importance of attending the University of Pennsylvania. But what motivated their loyalty?

I happened to join the Annenberg School as a research assistant and began my teaching career at the same time as these students enrolled in its Master of Arts in Communication program. The School was new, and this was an exciting time for all of us. The School has become more academic since and the world of media has changed quite radically, which made me most curious as to what happened to the graduates after they completed their education. I was looking forward seeing them again and hearing their stories.

During this reunion of the ASC Class of 1965, someone recovered a 1965 *Life Magazine* article about U.S. graduate education, largely because it mentioned the Annenberg School in passing. Under the headline of "The Great Grad School Gold Rush" the article claimed that the current population of graduate students was growing merely because of the increasing availability of funds for education. It went on to report that most graduate students were so comfortable that they didn't see the need to do anything else. What a putdown of graduate education and everything we hoped to accomplish! But worse, when flipping through the pages of that issue of *Life Magazine, almost all women looked like fashion models whose sole purpose was to make products and services appear attractive.*

These were the popular stereotypes that educated women faced. The opportunity to see in print what the 1960s public celebrated made me aware that we all live in the present and that it takes images of the past to disclose what we blindly accepted then.

In the 1960s, academic education was far from an established path to jobs for graduates. A Master of Arts degree in Communication was quite unknown and graduates with such a degree had to struggle to explain their acquired competencies. Many had to start at jobs far below what they had studied for and yearned to excel in. For women graduates, double difficulties awaited them. Not only had they dared to choose an academic education – often against advice of family members – but also they faced unbelievable gender prejudices, harassment, and disrespect. The experiences these graduates shared were plainly shocking by contemporary standards. Glass ceilings were barely above crawl spaces.

The stories published in *On the Cusp – The Women of Penn '64* reveal the unbelievable preconceptions women faced after leaving the University. Not that academic life was entirely free of gender issues. The University had a Dean of Women. Despite her conservative advice for women to seek jobs in nursing and teaching, most schools did not merely provide a safe haven to explore prescribed subjects; instead they encouraged women to think outside the box. In 1965, one third of Annenberg graduates were women. They were welcomed and excelled without discrimination. The University was led by two remarkable woman presidents, the current one even more outstanding than the first. Penn admitted the brightest students and provided an education that expanded women's aspirations beyond expectations and gave them the strength to pursue them against existing odds.

The Penn Class of 1964 had only 385 women graduates. These few women alumni developed their own companies, sat on corporate boards, held professorships at important universities, and made significant contributions. To share their stories and reflect on how they managed to persist in this changing world is what brought both Penn and Annenberg graduates together after 50 years and gave birth to the idea of this book.

As a critical communication scholar that I have become since, I was most eager to learn what these women took away from their alma mater, and what enabled them to unstoppably create not only novel paths in pursuit of their own missions but also the spaces for other women to go even further. Meeting again after fifty years, it became clear what a remarkable group of graduates – especially of women – they were, what they grew from the seeds that the University had planted in their lives, and what their stories can encourage us to dare to do today.

179

Afterword by Judith von Seldeneck

Founder, Diversified Search
Founder, Forum of Executive Women

From my earliest days, I was athletic, a sports enthusiast and very competitive. I wanted to be the best, and nothing was going to stop me. There must have been a commonality in our upbringing that made the women of the 1960s so competitive. Back then, women weren't very helpful to each other. They often didn't wish each other well.

When I graduated from the University of North Carolina in 1964, I ended up in Washington, D.C., working for Walter Mondale for ten years as his personal secretary. Back then women were nurses, teachers, or secretaries. I went to law school at night, thinking that might be a good way to eventually break out of the secretary mode.

In 1974, I married and moved to Philadelphia. That's when I began a search firm that placed women from non-profit organizations into for-profit corporations. Large government contractors and companies doing business with the federal government were reminded by the office of contract compliance that they would have to do a better job hiring "women and minorities" if they wanted to get government contracts. So we visited with large companies and other government contractors and said, "Tell us about your professional jobs, and we'll find you qualified women."

By 1977, there were so many outstanding women in the Philadelphia area market that my business partner and I started the Forum of Executive Women for businesswomen. We originally set a maximum of 75 women who could be members. Today the membership is nearly 500, with no maximum. There are CEOs, partner level accountants and lawyers, heads of not-for-profits, and government officials.

But by the late 1970s into the 1980s, it was becoming apparent that women were becoming isolated. They would be placed in high-level jobs, but had no other people they could go talk to—to understand how to best succeed in their jobs. Men played golf or went out for beers, but often women weren't included.

Women just didn't seem to be able to figure out the right way to go about making their case. The tactics of marching, demonstrating, burning bras, and shouting just did not resonate and, in hindsight, there probably was a better way that would have gotten women much further along a lot faster; I believe we really did ourselves a disservice. In the last few decades companies have become much smarter about doing succession planning at the board level, but the progress has been painstakingly slow. Public scrutiny and increased active investor interest in board composition is helping to accelerate better diversity representation.

Women in business have come a long way since the sixties, but obviously not as far as we would like. Some of the old traditional obstacles remain, but they are dwindling with passage of time. There has never been a better time for women who truly want to excel in their careers to do so. But they have to be willing to make their careers their top priority, and commit the time and energy and go toe to toe with the best and the brightest!

There are no free rides; there never have been. But the highways are newly paved and the vehicles equipped to excel at a record pace. Women now need to step up and get behind the controls.

APPENDIX

Penn's Heritage — America's first university

The University of Pennsylvania dates its founding to 1740, when
prominent evangelist George
Whitefield had the idea of
building a Philadelphia charity
school that would double as a
house of worship. In 1749,
Benjamin Franklin, inventor and
future founding father of the
United States, published his essay
urging the education of children
of the gentry and working class
alike. Franklin's educational
aims — to train young people for
leadership in business,
government and public service —
were innovative for the time.
Those aims convinced 24 of
Philadelphia's leading citizens to
become trustees for the Academy
and Charitable School in the

Benjamin Franklin

Province of Pennsylvania which opened its doors in 1751. Its program of
study was more like the modern liberal arts curriculum. Franklin served
as president until 1755 and continued to serve as a trustee until his death
in 1790.

Penn's claim as the first *university* in the United States is based on the
1765 founding of the first medical school in America, making Penn the
first institution to offer both undergraduate and professional education.
The 1779 charter made Penn the first American institution of higher
learning to take the name of "university." Although Harvard (chartered
in 1650), William and Mary (1693), and Yale (1701) preceded Penn, they
were organized on the plans of traditional English colleges.

By the 1860s, the University had outgrown its space in downtown
Philadelphia so, in 1872, the trustees built a new campus in the then
street-car suburb of West Philadelphia. Now, Penn's 302-acre campus
has more than 200 buildings and many notable landmarks, including the
nation's first student union (Houston Hall, 1894) and first double-decker
college football stadium (Franklin Field, 1924).

Franklin Field

Its many subsequent firsts include: the first collegiate business school (Wharton, 1881, endowed by Industrial Age ironmaster Joseph Wharton); the world's first electronic, large-scale, general-purpose digital computer (ENIAC, 1946); and the first woman president of an Ivy League institution, Judith Rodin (1994); as well as the first female Ivy League president to succeed another female, Amy Gutmann (2004).

Commencing in the second half of the twentieth century, the University of Pennsylvania grew in size as well as in stature as a celebrated research

university. Its role in setting standards for urban renewal by city-based universities in the postwar redevelopment and expansion played an important part in the evolving profile of American cities.

Ruth Lichterman (left) and Marlyn Wescoff, two of the six women who programmed ENIAC, the first fully electronic computer, in the 1940s. U.S. Army photo.

The campus grappled with twentieth-century racial tensions, gender inequality, labor conflicts, and economic retrenchment. The key policies and initiatives of the administrations led by presidents Gaylord Harnwell, Martin Meyerson, Sheldon Hackney and Judith Rodin shaped campus life in this turbulent era leading to the twenty-first century.

History of Women at Penn

Women were always present in the student body at Penn, but at first only in the Charity School for children, not in the College or professional schools. When the Charity School closed in 1877, "The Trustees redirected the income of the Charity School trust to collegiate scholarships for young men and to instruction for 'female students' so far as the Provost thought appropriate at the University." The women could not earn undergraduate degrees in their then-status as "special students" in the Towne Scientific School.

Not until 1914 when the School of Education was established were bachelor's degrees conferred on women. In 1933, the College of Liberal Arts for Women was founded and admitted its first female students in a degree-granting liberal arts program, to be instructed by an all-male faculty.

College Hall was the first building on the West Philadelphia campus. The building housed almost all of the college functions, including the library, classrooms, laboratories and offices. In recent years, the building has been the home of the President, Provost, School of Arts and Sciences, the Department of History and the Undergraduate Admissions Office. The building's significance in the history of collegiate architecture has been recognized by U.S. Department of Interior by placing it on the National Registry of Historic Places and in the University of Pennsylvania Historic District.

Highlights of Three Centuries of Women at Penn

1751: Advertisement in the *Pennsylvania Gazette:*

> *"As the Scheme formed by the Gentlemen of Philadelphia, for the regular Education of their Sons, has been happily carried into execution; the Ladies excited by the laudable example, are solicitous that their Daughters too might be instructed in the some Parts of Learning, as they are taught in the Academy."*

1876: Two women, Gertrude Klein Pierce and Anna Lockhart Flanigen, enroll as special students in the Towne Scientific School. They are the first women to complete a collegiate course of study at Penn although they are *not* eligible for a degree.

1880: Mary Alice Bennett, M.D., is granted a Doctor of Philosophy degree, becoming the first woman to earn a degree at the University of Pennsylvania.

1883: Penn Law School graduate Caroline Burnham Kilgore, LL.B, becomes the first woman to be admitted to the Pennsylvania Bar.

1890: Col. Joseph M. Bennett donates two townhouses at 34th and Walnut Streets "to encourage and enable...coeducation of women or girls."

1900: The Women's Club is formed "To promote social interests among the women students and especially to provide...for the undergraduates an opportunity for college life."

1912: Women's rights activist Alice Paul receives her Doctor of Philosophy in Sociology degree before founding the National Woman's Party, which fought for passage of the 19th Amendment to the Constitution, ratified in 1920, making it legal for women to vote.

1919: The Graduate School of Medicine is founded and matriculation is open to both men and women.

1920: The School of Fine Arts is founded, although the course in architecture does not admit women.

1921: Margaret Majer becomes the first coach of women's athletic teams, including women's basketball, gymnastics, softball, swimming and tennis.

1925: The third Bennett Hall opens at 34th and Walnut Streets, home to the School of Education and the Graduate School of Arts and Sciences.

The Furness Library, now officially known as the Fisher Fine Arts Library. Designed by the acclaimed Philadelphia architect Frank Furness (1839–1912), the red sandstone, brick-and-terra-cotta Venetian Gothic giant was built to be the primary library of the University, and to house its archeological collection. The cornerstone was laid in October 1888, construction was completed in late 1890, and the building was dedicated in February 1891. The building was designated a National Historic Landmark in 1985.

1933: The College of Liberal Arts for Women is founded and admits women students only, offering a full-time, four-year, liberal arts, undergraduate degree program.

1945: Helen Octavia Dickens is the first African American woman to earn the M.Sc. (Med.) degree at Penn.

1951: A total of 4,234 women are enrolled in 24 different academic programs. The majority of women students (2,273 or 53.68%) continue to attend classes on a part-time basis, but the number enrolled in courses leading to degrees has increased substantially (2,441 or 57.65%).

1954: The Wharton School and the School of Engineering and Applied Science admit women to the undergraduate program.

1960: Dr. Rebecca Jean Brownlee becomes the first woman to be appointed dean of the College of Liberal Arts for Women, the third woman to be named an academic dean at Penn.

1961: New women's residence, Hill College House (originally Hill Hall Women's Dormitories), opens.

Hill College House is an internationally recognized architectural landmark. It was designed in 1958 by Eero Saarinen, who designed, among other buildings, the St. Louis Arch, the Kennedy Airport in New York and Dulles Airport in Washington, D.C. Hill was originally designed to be a women's dormitory. The drawbridge, moat, and spiked-fence motif outside was intended to keep men out. Today, Hill is co-ed and, with almost 500 residents, it is one of Penn's largest college houses.

1969: In September, Judith Linda Teller (B.S. in Econ., 1971) is elected the first woman Editor-in-Chief of *The Daily Pennsylvanian*, the independent daily student newspaper founded in 1885.

1971: An Equal Opportunity Office is established at Penn to develop and implement a University-wide Affirmative Action Plan, "to ensure equality for women and for members of the minority groups."

1976: 100 years after women first enrolled in the College as "special students," the University becomes fully co-educational.

1983: Stephanie A.J. Dangel is named the first Penn woman recipient of a Rhodes Scholarship.

1994: Judith Rodin (A.B., 1966), M.A., Ph.D., becomes the seventh President and Chief Executive of the University of Pennsylvania, and is

the first woman to serve as President of an Ivy League institution. Rodin is the immediate past president of the Rockefeller Foundation in New York. She previously served as a provost of Yale University.

During Rodin's administration (1994-2004), the Chronicle of Higher Education refers to Penn's progress as a "national model of constructive town-gown inter-action and partnership."

Judith Rodin

> "The incredible change that the University of Pennsylvania experienced under Judith Rodin's tenure mirrored that of the city of Philadelphia. As Penn transformed the face of West Philadelphia and helped the city meet its educational and economic challenges, the city itself became more livable and a better place. President Rodin's reach not only transformed a great university but helped in the revival of one of America's oldest and proudest cities."
>
> Edward G. Rendell
> Former Governor, Commonwealth of Pennsylvania

2001: Penn alumnae celebrate the 125th anniversary of the admission of women to Penn. The two-day event honors Penn women and recognizes their many notable achievements.

2004: Dr. Amy Gutmann, the Provost of Princeton University, is named the eighth President and Chief Executive of the University of Pennsylvania.

2016: Dr. Amy Gutman's contract is extended to 2021.

References

Becoming Penn: The Pragmatic American University, 1950-2001, John L. Puckett and Mark Frazier Lloyd, University of Pennsylvania Press, 2015.

University of Pennsylvania Archives & Records Center, esp.
   http://www.archives.upenn.edu/histy/features/women/chrontext.html

About the Authors

Anne Sceia Klein received a B.S. degree in Economics in 1964 from Penn's Wharton School and received her master's degree in 1965 from Penn's Annenberg School for Communication. She served on her 50th undergraduate class reunion committee and chaired her graduate school's 50th reunion.

Anne is the founder of Anne Klein Communications Group, LLC (AKCG). She played a leading role in the public relations arena for five decades. Anne has received numerous awards for her outstanding achievements and contributions to her profession and to business. In 2006, she was inducted into Rowan University's Public Relations Hall of Fame, and in 2004, Anne was inducted into the Philadelphia Public Relations Association's Hall of Fame. In 2017, she was honored with a Lifetime Achievement Award from the Philadelphia chapter of the Public Relations Society of America.

Under Anne's leadership, AKCG won dozens of awards for excellence in public relations. She is the author of chapters in six books and countless articles on PR.

Anne Sceia Klein and Vilma Barr

Vilma Barr received a B.S. in Marketing Management from Drexel University, Philadelphia, and completed a joint graduate program in Organizational Studies and Urban Studies and Planning at the Massachusetts Institute of Technology.

She has written, co-authored, and edited 17 non-fiction books on business, the built environment, and art-related subjects, including retail store design, radio station design, architecture, photography, marketing professional services, and sales management. She also serves as a book coach to develop content with experts in their field of specialization for book-length works.

Her editorial consulting firm, Barr Publications & Editorial Services, Philadelphia, specializes in creating and implementing promotional strategies for service organizations. As a contributing editor, her columns and feature articles appear in U.S. and international professional periodicals, combining text and illustrations on topics relating to commercial lighting applications and to retail store design and construction. She has been appointed Collection Editor of the Sustainability Group of books, published by Momentum Press for professionals who design the built environment.